FORT
TOWNS
OF
FRANCE

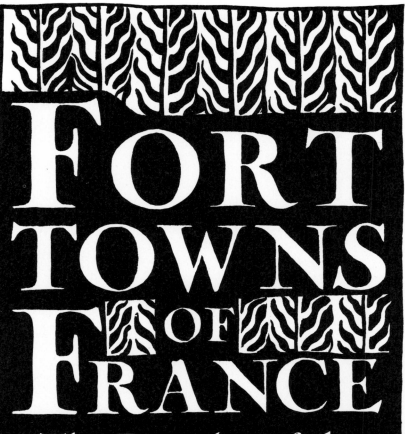

FORT TOWNS OF FRANCE

The Bastides of the Dordogne & Aquitaine

by
James Bentley

Tauris Parke Books

Published by Tauris Parke Books
45 Bloomsbury Square
London WC1A 2HY
in association with KEA Publishing Services Ltd., London

Text and captions © 1993 James Bentley
Photographs © 1993 Francesco Venturi/KEA Publishing Services Ltd.

The Cataloguing in Publication Data for this book is
available from the British Library, London

ISBN 1-85043-608-8

Designed by Barbara Mercer
Original artwork by Julian Bingley
Map drawn by Andras Bereznay
Typesetting by August Filmsetting, St Helens
Colour separation by Fabbri, Milan, Italy
Printed by Fabbri, Milan, Italy

Contents

Acknowledgements

The author and photographer would like to express their thanks for the help of Mme Marie-Yvonne Jolley of the Comité Régional de Tourisme d'Aquitaine, and of the Centre d'Etudes des Bastides, 5 place de la Fontaine, Villefranche de Rouergue. Also Britanny Ferries and Mme Marie-Yvonne Holley of the Regional Committee for Tourism, Rue René Cassen, 33000 Bordeaux, and Antonio Russo.

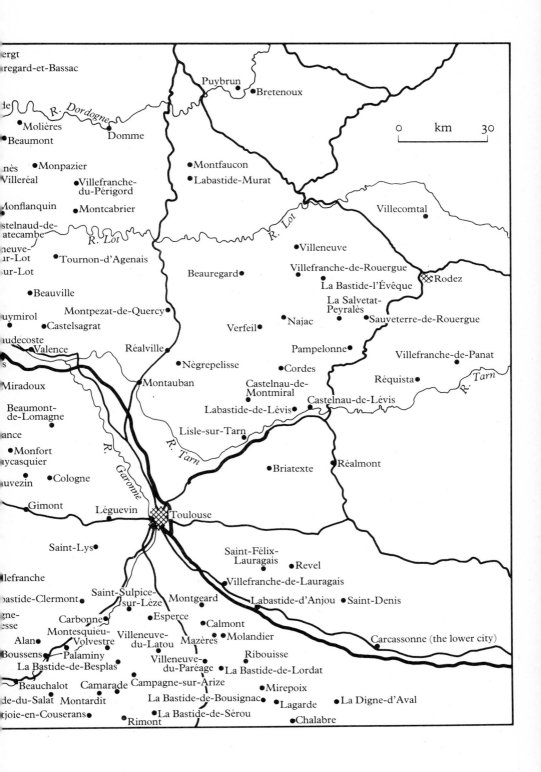

Introduction

Travellers and tourists in south-west France frequently come across remarkable walled medieval towns. Once inside the walls they find a yet more entrancing phenomenon. Streets crossing each other at right angles are flanked by ancient houses. Built out of local materials, whether wattle and daub, stone, brick or a mixture of these, sometimes half-timbered, these houses are laid out in clearly designed parcels of land, all either square or rectangular, all the same size.

Little alleyways run off between the houses, which all converge on a market square. Around the square the houses almost always jut out over covered walks, opening on to the market place by means of pointed, round or square arcades, sometimes a beguiling mixture of all three. Brick pillars, wooden posts or stone arches support the houses above these arcades.

At the centre of most of the market places rises a medieval open market hall. Some are huge, such as the one at Cordes, whose pantiled roof, resting on stone pillars and supported by a fretwork of carpentry, fills virtually the whole square, some are set alongside the houses on one side of the square, some of these market halls carry on top the town hall. They date from the very foundation of such fortified towns. If the visitor is fortunate, it will be market day, when colourful awnings shade the stalls of the local farmers whose ancestors have been bringing their produce to these markets for some six centuries or more. To one side of the market place, usually a little way off as if to shun the money changers, rises a superb medieval church. Humbler, equally necessary features are the well, the fountain and the communal wash house.

Technically these fortified towns are known as bastides, a word which originally signified any kind of stronghold but came to have this particular application in the thirteenth century. The first, the astonishingly beautiful bastide of Cordes, was created in 1222 by Count Raymond VII of Toulouse. All of them were founded within the space of 150 years, either by the French or by the English. Maybe six hundred of them were founded in that short space of time. Three hundred or so remain, many of them completely unspoilt.

The bastides endured the Hundred Years War, several of them pillaged in 1355 by the Black Prince (who has a medieval house named after him in the bastide of Monflanquin). In the sixteenth and early seventeenth centuries they survived the vicious wars of religion. Occasionally a bastide lacks a medieval church, because the Huguenots pulled it down. More often the fortifications have gone, dismantled by Catholics determined that the bastides should never again become fortresses of the Protestants.

Though they speak to us of the Middle Ages, bastides are not marooned in the past. Most of them are animated spots. These were completely new towns in the thirteenth and fourteenth centuries, and the men and women who founded them needed to attract people to live inside them, indeed to build them. They did so by offering a range of privileges hitherto scarcely seen in France. Among those privileges was the right to hold regular markets and fairs, which still continue.

The gazetteer which constitutes the last section of this book lists the market days and the numerous fairs which have survived from the Middle Ages and still enliven these ancient towns and cities.

New towns are by definition founded outside the existing centres of population, and many of the bastides are no exception to this rule. Over the centuries the forests and wildernesses in which they once stood have been cleared and made fertile by those who lived within the walls. Today the market stalls inside these bastides are loaded with the specialities which each region derives from its lush surrounding fields: the plums of Villeneuve-sur-Lot, for example, which become the celebrated *pruneau d'Agen*; the liqueurs of the bastides of the Armagnac; the strawberries of Vergt;

the force-fed geese and ducks to which the bastide of Mazères dedicates a whole festival at the beginning of December.

For obvious reasons, wherever possible a bastide was sited near a river, a feature that has made many of them ideal leisure centres in the twentieth century. Some are blessed even more: Damazan, for instance, nowadays exploits its eight hectare lake for water sports.

The great ones who founded these bastides — such as the English queen Eleanor of Provence, the kings of Navarre, the counts of Toulouse, the seneschals of the rulers of England and France, and Gaston Fébus who likened himself to the sun-god — often possessed strong personalities, and this book aims to evoke those personalities.

The founders were also responding to the unique needs of a moment in medieval French history. Bastides were their answer to those needs. To understand them we must step back in history first of all to the savage years of the Albigensian crusade.

Land of
Heretics

The history of some of the finest fortified towns of south-west France begins with a murder. At dawn on 15 January, 1208, a delegate of Pope Innocent III named Pierre de Castelnau was assassinated close by Saint-Gilles, which lies on the route to Arles beside the River Rhône.

With the authority of the pope, Pierre de Castelnau had publicly excommunicated Count Raymond VI of Toulouse and the two men had violently quarrelled. Pierre then set off for the Rhône with the intention of returning to Rome. Raymond pursued him, perhaps seeking some reconciliation, but before they met, one of the count's servants murdered the legate. Hearing the news, the pope fell into a silent rage which lasted two days. Then he announced a crusade against the French heretics, the Cathars (or Albigensians), among whose leaders was Count Raymond.

The pope was an Italian, Lotario dei Segni, elected in 1198. Learned and vigorous, Innocent III was also a master politician. Believing that the church was superior to the state, he successfully intervened in political matters, for instance crowning Otto IV Holy Roman Emperor in 1209, excommunicating him the following year when Otto presumed to seize church lands and invade Sicily, and with the aid of France and the German nobility managing to have him deposed in 1215. In England he alienated King John by appointing an archbishop of Canterbury against the king's wishes, and then brought the monarch to heel by excommunicating him and putting the country under interdict until John submitted.

In south-west France, Innocent was faced with the problem that many of the citizens cared little for excommunication, for they were, in their own eyes, already part of the true church, having espoused the teachings of the Cathars. Theirs was a new religion, and socially a bizarre one. It derived from the oriental cults of Zarathustra, notions brought to France by merchants and by the heretical Bulgarian Bishop Nicetas of Constantinople, who arrived to address a congress held at Saint-Félix-de-Caraman near Toulouse in 1167. Many of these heretics flourished from the cloth trade, exporting from Narbonne to the Levant, and their contacts with the east helped to re-inforce the new doctrines.

From these sources, many in the Midi came to believe in the duality of good and evil. The earthly realm, they were convinced, belonged entirely to Satan — and with it the Catholic Church. Only the Cathars (a word deriving from the Greek for 'pure') belonged to God.

Naturally, in spite of their rejection of the material world, even the most convinced Cathars had to eat, but their leaders were vegetarians, rejecting even milk and eggs although accepting fish. Carnal intercourse seemed also of the devil, since children merely prolonged the life of this evil world. Suicide was no sin, for it brought the end of the world nearer. As for the sacraments of the Church, these too were dangerous, since they involved earthly things such as water in baptism and bread and wine at the Eucharist.

Soon, however, the Cathar community divided itself into two classes: the 'perfects' and the rest. What of the 'perfects'? In 1302 a shepherd of Montaillou in the Pyrenees asked this question of two Cathars in the village and was told:

> They are men like the others! Their flesh, their bones, their shape, their faces are all exactly like those of other men! But they are the only ones to walk in the ways of justice and truth which the Apostles followed. They do not lie. They do not take what belongs to others. Even if they found gold and silver lying in their path, they would not 'lift' it unless someone made them a present of it. Salvation is better achieved in the faith of these men called heretics than in any other faith.

But the rest of Cathar humanity, while admiring the 'perfects', preferred to put off the rigour of Cathar morality till the very last moment. Their excuse was a kind of last sacrament known as the 'consolamentum', which at the very end of their lives gave them entry into the realm of the spirit.

Only then, in the presence of the 'perfects', did they commit themselves wholly to God and the Gospel. Only then did they promise to eat only fish or vegetable dishes cooked in oil, to abstain from lying, swearing oaths and indulging in carnal intercourse. Then a holy book (presumably a copy of the New Testament) was laid on the Cathar's head, and at last the man or woman became a 'perfect'.

Many Cathars thought it wise to submit to this rite in times of war, in case the men died in battle and the women and children were killed by the enemy. In case they survived, they also were obliged to promise to remain faithful to the Cathar community, on pain of death by fire or drowning. Curiously enough, it seems that those who did survive were allowed if they wished to revert to their previous non-'perfect' status.

In consequence, these less-than-perfect Cathars found themselves in the happy position of sinning while remaining certain of forgiveness and an entry into the spiritual realm at the point of death. Cathar priests and laity blithely comitted adultery, took mistresses, cheated each other out of sheep, indulged in family revenge and occasionally murdered good Catholics, restrained from these acts only by imprisonment and sometimes by being burned at the stake.

The heresy flourished most of all in upper Languedoc, and especially around Albi which indeed gave the Cathars their alternative name: Albigenses. Here the Catholic Church had only a feeble hold, where no monastic reform had penetrated and such religious foundations as existed were weak in both numbers and intellect. As one Cathar observed in Ascou near Aix-les-Thermes, 'The priests teach people very little. Fewer than half their parishioners go to hear them preach or understand anything of what they say.' In such circumstances, by the mid-twelfth century the heresy had recruited the upper classes and the poor alike.

These anarchists were socially as well as theologically dangerous. In 1176 an Orthodox council held at Albi condemned them. The Lateran Council repeated the condemnation three years later – to no avail. The heresy remained firmly implanted in such places as Carcassonne, Toulouse, Albi, Montauban, Cordes. One bishop of Albi was virtually imprisoned in his cathedral by these heretics. When his successor Bernard de Castenet, equally anxious about the English who were marauding in the neighbour-hood, decided to restore the building, he created a house of God which resembles a vast, defensive fortress. Surrounded by mid-fourteenth-century fortifications which have now disappeared, Albi was taken only once in succeeding centuries.

Among the heretics were powerful men. From the early twelfth cen-tury the counts of Toulouse had been convinced Cathars. By the time of Pope Innocent III the cult included among its members not only Count Raymond VI of Toulouse, but also his nephew Raymond Trencavel, who was the young viscount of Béziers, Carcassonne and Albi. Another powerful Cathar was Raymond-Roger, count of Foix, whose wife actually ran a convent for the 'perfects'. Innocent III, initially unwilling to try to convert them by force of arms, was well aware of the ignorance of the Languedoc clergy, 'mute dogs who don't even know how to bark', as he decribed them (adding for good measure that Archbishop Berengar of Narbonne 'knew no other god than money and had a purse where his heart should have been'). His initial aim was to bring these heretics back to Catholicism by good example.

The greatest exponent of this technique was a Castilian named Dom-ingo Guzmàn, better known today as Saint Dominic, who created an order of preaching friars dedicated to poverty, humility and charity. Dressed in a simple white robe, in contrast to the black gowns of the 'perfects', Dominic and six companions were welcomed at Toulouse by the Catholic Bishop Foulques in 1206. Then he and his companions set out to walk through the country in the hope of converting Cathars. At Car-cassonne they preached against the heretics and charitably disputed with them for six days. At what is now the bastide of Limoux beside the River Aude he founded a church, dedicated to Saint Martin of Tours. It still stands there. At Pamiers in the valley of the Ariège he and his companions succeeded in converting a sizeable number of Cathars to orthodox Chris-tianity. Elsewhere they often failed.

Around 1209, Dominic installed himself as parish priest at Fan-jeaux, a walled, hilltop village set today amid broom trees and windmills. Founded by the Romans, its name derives from a temple to Jupiter (Fanum Jovis). Little has changed since the Middle Ages. Even the house where Saint Dominic lived for nine years still stands. The late twelfth-century church preserves a seven-arched Romanesque doorway through which he must often have passed. In Fanjeaux, too, you can still visit the former cloisters and chapter house of the Dominican convent, which date respectively from the fourteenth and fifteenth centuries. The ancient market hall was built a century later.

When Dominic arrived the place was a centre of Catharism. Two years previously the Cathar Bishop Guilhabert de Castres, had ordained Esclarmonde de Foix as a 'perfect' here, in the presence of his brother Count Raymond-Roger and the whole nobility of the region. A Cathar cross still stands on the bridge into the town. Dominic himself was initially in some danger at Fanjeaux. Once two Cathars lay in wait to kill him, but when they saw his holy face they could not bear to. Eventually his measured, logical preaching brought several Cathars to Catholicism. Nearby, at Prouille, he set up a convent for nine women, all of them former Cathars. Their ideal was the basis of Dominicanism: prayer; trained preachers; and shelters for those who had chosen to shun the world for a better life.

Although many were converted from Catharism by the friars, ultimately their mission was a failure. Their nearest approach to a serious dialogue with the Cathars occurred in the spring of 1207 at the town of Montréal, where several noble ladies lived in a house of the 'perfects'. Montréal welcomed from the Catholic camp Dominic, Bishop Diego of Osma, the soon-to-be-murdered papal legate Pierre de Castelnau and his colleague Raoul of the abbey of Fontefroide. Their opponents were led by the scholarly Cathar Bishop Guilhabert de Castres. The heretics lost the contest, albeit in a quaint fashion. They demanded that their various writings be put to the test of fire. Repairing to Fanjeaux, they threw Cathar and Catholic books into the flames. Every Cathar book was instantly consumed, while Dominic's manuscripts leapt out of the fire on to a beam in the church (which still shows traces of charring). At this, numerous Cathars converted to Catholicism.

In a few other spots Cathars and Catholics managed to live together in harmony. Surprisingly, one was Albi, which, especially in the thirteenth century under the benign rule of Bishop Guilhem Peyre, who was also lord of the city, was a rare centre of tolerance. Another was the hilltop village of Saint-Michel-de-Lanès at the western extremity of the *département* of the Aude, where in the Romanesque church which still stands there each religious community took turns to celebrate its own cult.

For Innocent III these accommodations and the few conversions brought about by Dominic were not enough. Not far north of Dominic's French home, Cathars and Catholics were at odds in the still lovely medieval village of Villeneuve-le-Comptal. The saint went to preach there – to no avail. With the murder of his legate and the failure of Dominic's mission, the pope determined on the total extermination of Catharism, and for this purpose appealed to the king of France to march against them. King Philippe Auguste declined the honour, but the crusade was taken up by the lords of Burgundy, of Normandy and of the Ile de France. From the Ile de France came the formidable Simon de Montfort, earl of Leicester. Like the other nobles, his motives were mixed: they were certainly attracted by the promise of papal remission of all sins; the ease with which their forces could overwhelm the flimsier troops of the Midi; and the booty which would surely be theirs. They scented potentially rich lands to conquer. For Simon, too, Cathars were 'servants of the devil'.

Twenty thousand Catholic knights descended on the Rhône valley in 1209. Speedily, Raymond VI decided to convert to Catholicism and put himself at their head. At odds with his nephew Raymond Trencavel, he sacked Béziers on 22 July, massacring thousands of heretics – and it seems, several thousand Catholics too – including some who had vainly sought sanctuary in the church of the Madeleine. Abbot Arnaud-Amalric of

Cîteaux is said to have urged, 'Kill them all. God will recognize which are which.' After pillaging Béziers, the crusaders set it on fire, and the city blazed for two days.

On 26 July the crusaders marched towards the city of Carcassonne, a hotbed of Catharism. Its lord, the 24-year-old Raymond-Roger Trencavel (who happened to be Catholic), hurriedly summoned knights to his aid, while his workmen strengthened the defences of the suburbs and the already superb fortifications of the city. Then (in the account of Pierre des Vaux de Carnay who was present at the siege on the side of the Catholics), 'our forces approached the ramparts of one of the suburbs and launched an attack, at which the people defended themselves with such courage that our troops retreated from the moat under a hail of stones.' One knight lay in the moat with a broken leg for hours, because nobody dared rescue him. Then the crusaders set up their huge catapults and with them partly demolished the walls of the suburbs. 'Next with some difficulty the crusaders brought to the base of the walls a four-wheeled chariot, covered with cowhide, to conceal the sappers who planned to destroy the ramparts,' the chronicler continues. 'Soon the enemy had destroyed the chariot, but the sappers had taken shelter in a niche they had already dug.' The outer wall collapsed at daybreak.

The walled city was still intact. The crusaders decided to withdraw, at least temporarily. At this Carcassonne's defenders rushed out and killed any invader they could catch, before retreating back to the town. Instead of continuing the siege, the Catholics decided to negotiate. Eventually Raymond-Roger offered himself as their prisoner, provided that the city was spared. Imprisoned in a dungeon in his own Carcassonne, he died on 10 November, 1209.

Raymond VI's swift conversion from Catharism to Catholicism was matched by other curious alliances. Perceiving his patrimony threatened, he sought the help of the Catholic King Pedro II of Aragon, who had no wish to see the Languedoc invested by the northern French. Pedro, alas, was killed on 12 September, 1213, at the battle of Muret, leading his knights in the face of a brutal attack by the French.

Simon de Montfort seemed invincible. Aimery, lord of Montréal, submitted to him after the fall of Minerve, offering de Montfort the fortified town of Montréal as well as neighbouring Lurac, provided that in return Aimery was given land in the plain. Next de Montfort attacked nearby Lavaur, which Aimery attempted to defend along with his sister Dame Guiraude. The siege was successful, and de Montfort presented Dame Guiraude to his soldiers as a plaything, before having her flung alive into a well which was then filled with stones. Such cruelty was well rewarded by his church; in February 1211, Dominic himself baptized de Montfort's daughter, Pétronille, in the church of the château at Montréal (situated on the highest spot in the town, a place now named l'Espérou which commands magnificent views).

At Fanjeaux, too, de Montfort was spectacularly successful. On his very approach in August 1209 the Cathar citizens and their bishop fled, most of them taking refuge in the temple fortress of Montségur, which had been built on a 1207-metre peak north-east of Villeneuve-sur-Lot around 1204 by Ramon de Péreilla at the behest of the Cathar clergy.

Simon de Montfort never took Montségur. Making Fanjeaux a base for his campaigns, he struck up a friendship with Dominic. Already his proselytizing techniques had proved far different from those of the saint. De Montfort's energy was prodigious and his effect deadly. First he secured his base at Carcassonne. The Trencavel family had become lords of both Béziers and Carcassonne, and in the latter city Roger de Trencavel had offered protection to Cathars. Simon took Carcassonne in 1209 and made it his main headquarters. His troops were stationed at the château of Pen-nautier, to the north-west of the city (a town which today has lost most of its fortifications, save for some vestiges of the wall and a defensive tower). Soon they had taken the strategically important and still beautiful city of Limoux from the Trencavels. Further south-west, after a siege lasting three days, they conquered the immensely powerful château of Puivert, its vestiges still imposing, the walls defended by round and square towers, the keep rising to 35 metres.

Thenceforth Simon de Montfort littered the region of the bastides with ruined châteaux and fortresses, captured and sacked by him, as well as with the evocative remains of the towns and villages he invested. Today many of these spots are exquisite – romantic survivals of the Middle Ages. At the hamlet of Clermont-sur-Laquet in the *département* of the Aude, for instance, are a few remains of the Cathar fortress he demolished. Moving north-east, his forces wrecked the little town of Homps, once an important headquarters of the Knights Hospitallers.

De Montfort took the château of Alairac in the Aude in 1210; the château no longer exists, but the village still clusters around its Romanesque parish church. By 1211 he held the fortress of La Pomarède in the Aude, its keep standing to this day. Further north, he took the château of Saint-Martin-Laguépie in the same year. Montmaur, a fortress built, as its name implies to repel the Saracens, was in de Montfort's hands by 1212. Though protected by a fortress with a newly built keep and a double ring of walls, Roquefort-sur-Garonne fell to him the following year. Saint-Couade-d'Aude, another perched and fortified town, was not taken by him till 1215, in which year he also forced the submission of the fortress and town of Montlaur.

During these campaigns de Montfort's brother Philippe prosecuted the crusade further north. Castres had been an important Cathar stronghold since the twelfth century. Philippe took it in 1209. Simon himself soon led his forces north, sacking the Cathar priory of Saint-Pierre-de-Salvetat at Mont-dragon north-west of Castres. The Orthodox pushed still further north in pursuit of heretics. Soon Simon de Montfort's troops were investing what are now the *départements* of the Lot and the Dordogne. At Gindou in the Lot they came upon and destroyed a Cathar fortress. In 1215, Bertrand de Card-aillac, lord of Larnagol in the same *département,* was forced to do homage to Simon. De Montfort took the château of Castelnaud-la-Chapelle in the Dordogne in 1214. In the same year he razed the château of Domme, which, much restored over the centuries, still rises starkly over the River Dordogne and now bears his name. The Cathars fought back by burning down the nearby abbey at Saint-Avit-Sénieur (which was rebuilt and once again destroyed in 1577, this time by French Protestants).

Simon de Montfort's campaigns were vicious. At Les Cassés in the Aude he took the fortress (which is now in ruins) and burned alive fifty heretics. At Termes, west of Limoux, the Cathars, led by Raymond de Termes, strenuously resisted his assaults in 1210; when the château here finally fell Simon had his enemy imprisoned in Carcassonne until his death. In 1211 his troops pillaged and sacked the city of Auterive in the Haute-Garonne. In the same year his troops pillaged the fortified village of Comigne, as well as demolishing most of the château at Coustaussa. Here only its curtain walls remain, built in the twelfth century, as well as the thirteenth century keep. Not content with this savagery, Simon then sacked the village of Coustaussa itself. He destroyed the town of Sorèze in 1212. When the seigneurs of Prayssac in the Lot refused to submit to him, de Montfort devastated their châteaux. Savagery towards those who refused to abjure their heresy con-tinued long after his death. In 1234, for instance, the lord of Crayssac in the Lot was slaughtered for resolutely espousing Catharism.

It would be an error to suppose that the Albigensian crusade was led solely by the de Montfort family. The bishops of Cahors were also vehement anti-heretics, in particular Guillaume de Cardaillac, who in 1209 captured Luzech, one of the four ancient baronies of Quercy, from the Cathars. In 1227 he defeated the Cathars of the town of Puy, renaming it in his own honour as Puy-l'Evêque. And the troops of Louis VIII himself destroyed the fortress town of Mas-Saintes-Puelles in the Aude, leaving standing only a few vestiges of its keep and walls. They also united Carcassonne with the French crown in 1229.

As evidence of the greed which matched the zeal of the crusaders, at times Simon de Montfort would even invest and take over a town or village that happened to be Catholic and not Cathar, for instance at Cabrespine in the Aude and at Bernis in the Gard in 1217. Among other nobles profiting financially from the fight against Catharism was Bertrand de Jean, to whom in 1214 the bishop of Cahors gave Les Junies, an important staging post on the road between Agen and Clermont-Ferrand, in gratitude for Bertrand's part in the Albigensian crusade.

Many Cathars were almost as redoubtable as Simon de Montfort. Cathar seigneurs from Rabat had owned La Bezole and its powerful fortress in the *département* of the Aude since 1176, and never lost it. North of Carcassonne, the Cathar stronghold of Lastours remains an astonishing sight. The erosion of the Orbiel gorge long ago left standing four rocky peaks, on which in the thirteenth and fourteenth centuries were built four mighty fortresses, connected by underground passages. De Montfort needed to make two assaults before its lord, Pierre Roger de Cabaret, surrendered.

On what is now the border between the *départements* of the Pyrénées-Orientales and the Aude, Cathars, protected by the magnificent fortress of Quéribus, lived securely at Maury and Cucignan, the Catholics driving them out only in 1255. Saint-Paul-Cap-de-Jac, in what is now the *département* of the Tarn, was taken from the Catholics by Count Raymond VII in 1228. Only in the same year was Nîmes finally taken over by the French crown, while the Cathar seigneur of Villevielle, a few kilometres south-west of that city, was not dispossessed of his town and lands until 1243. Louis IX did not conquer neighbouring Sommières until 1248.

Captured Cathar strongholds were never secure. Even Simon de Montfort realized this, and in 1211 was prevailed upon to attempt some reconciliation with Count Raymond VI of Toulouse. They met in the exquisite town of Ambialer (in the Tarn), to no avail. Two years later the Cathars were still on the offensive, and Raymond took back the town of Sainte-Foy-d'Aigrefeuille from the Catholic garrison. In 1219 he recaptured Baziège in the Haute-Garonne from Amaury de Montfort. Puilaurens, where the splendid remains of the château still overlook the town, was successfully defended against Simon de Montfort by its Cathar lord Guillaume de Peyrepetuse and remained in Cathar hands until the end of the Albigensian crusade.

Faced with the incessant assaults of the Orthodox, many Cathars proved remarkably resilient. Those living in the village of Missègre in the Aude preferred to destroy their homes rather than see them fall into enemy hands, abandoning their hilltop site and building a new village in the valley. A similar act of desperate bravery took place at Villemur-sur-Tarn. Seeing de Montfort's troops approaching, the Cathars set fire to their own town. When Simon de Montfort demolished the fortified Cathar village of Hautpoul, the survivors founded a new one a kilometre away which survives under the name Mazamet, below the ancient ruins of Hautpoul (where gravestones still exist with Cathar inscriptions). And it cost the royal crusader two attempts to conquer the virtually impregnable city of Rabastens, whose Romanesque church and ramparts still dominate the valley of the River Tarn.

The Cathars could be equally implacable in warfare as Simon de Montfort. In April 1211, Cathar troops at Montgey fell upon 5000 German troops, marching to swell the Catholic army, and massacred them all – at which Simon took revenge by destroying the château of Montgey and setting fire to the village.

Soon de Montfort was to meet a similar fate to that of his enemies. At a council held at Montpellier he persuaded the papal legates once more to excommunicate the once more recalcitrant Raymond VI of Toulouse, who fled to Genoa. The forces of the future King Louis the Pious then took

Toulouse and ravaged the population, before returning to the Ile de France. In the meantime Raymond VI and his son Raymond VII profited from Simon de Montfort's unpopularity to return from exile to Marseille. With many of the populace now on their side, they retook Toulouse. The earl of Leicester returned from the north, and on 25 June, 1218, as he besieged the city, a woman on the ramparts flung a rock at him. It struck him between the eyes and Simon de Montfort fell dead. His tomb, with a recumbent image of the knight, is in the south transept of the basilica of Saint Nazaire in the upper city of Carcassonne, though his corpse was later removed to Montfort l'Amaury just west of Paris.

Nearly all these protagonists were shortly to be gone from the scene. Excommunicated and dispossessed of his lands, Raymond VI died in 1222. Four years later King Louis IX of France, otherwise Saint Louis, led an army south which took first Avignon and then almost the whole of the Languedoc. Now Raymond VII of Toulouse was forced to kneel in his shirt on the forecourt of Notre-Dame-de-Paris to be publicly whipped and absolved of his heresy, promising Louis IX that he would purge the land of heretics. His daughter then married the king's brother, Alphonse de Poitiers. They died childless, and at last the Languedoc became undeniably part of the kingdom of France.

But Catharism was not yet conquered. At Cordes in the 1230s several of Dominic's preaching friars were thrown down a well. In 1233, Pope Gregory IX felt obliged to institute the Inquisition to combat the heresy. And the fortress at Montségur remained intact. In 1242 a group of Cathar soldiers on a sortie from Montségur murdered two Catholic inquisitors who were staying at Avignonnet-Lauragais under the supposed protection of the heretical governor of the château. (Their remains can still be seen in Toulouse cathedral.)

The murder enraged King Louis's mother, Blanche de Castille (who also had in mind the rich possibility of conquering a Mediterranean coastline and a prosperous commercial region). Describing the fortress of Montségur as 'the dragon's head' of Catharism, she ordered its conquest and destruction. Ramon de Péreilla, who built it, was still alive, and the defenders of the fortress were commanded by Pierre-Roger de Mirepoix, who had married his daughter Philippa. In June 1243 the seneschal of Carcassonne, Hugues d'Arcis, with the assistance of the warlike archbishop of Narbonne and bishop of Albi, besieged the fortress with a 6000 strong army. The Cathar stronghold, stocked with arms and provisions, finally fell to the Catholics on 14 March, 1244.

Even then, some 210 Cathars refused to renounce their faith. They were burnt alive. Ramon de Péreilla escaped with his life, but he saw his wife Corba, his daughters Esclarmonde and Arpaïs, and his mother in law Marquèsia de Lantar perish at the stake. For some time a royal garrison along with a Catholic chaplain held the fortress. Then Montségur was abandoned, to lie in ruins to this day. To the south-west the grim spot where the Cathars were burnt has been excavated.

By now some renegade Cathars had turned inquisitors, terrorizing their former fellow-believers. After 1250, it is true, few were burned to death, but many continued to be tortured. In spite of this savagery, Catharism lingered on in the Languedoc. In 1300 thirty-five suspected Cathar nobles were tried at Albi. Nineteen were found guilty and shackled for the rest of their lives. A Franciscan named Bernard Délicieux, based in Carcassonne, repeatedly attacked the Inquisition, only to find himself imprisoned for life in 1320. The last Cathar to be burned to death was a certain Bélibaste, who died at Villerouge-Termenès in 1321. 'Catharism was totally extirpated,' commented the historian Emmanuel Le Roy Ladurie. 'Its strange teaching, and the aureole of mystery and blood which surrounds its brief history have allowed it to be revived today as a source of poetical and philosophical inspiration.'

The legacy of Catharism and the Albigensian crusade is more than this, however. Paradoxically, heresy and vicious reprisal thus produced some of the most exquisite legacies of the Middle Ages, the bastides of south-west France.

In the four years before his death in 1222, Count Raymond VI of Toulouse had set about restoring his lands to prosperity. His successor, Count Raymond VII, who reigned until 1249, was acutely conscious that they also needed defending. North-west of Albi, in previous times the counts had relied on the fortress at Saint-Martin-Laguépie to defend their territories in this region. Today its ruins are a reminder that Simon de Montfort demolished it in 1211. A little further south-east, Count Raymond's predecessors had fortified the town of Saint-Marcel-Campes, which rises on a defensive site that had dominated the surrounding countryside since Merovingian times. In 1212, Simon de Montfort destroyed its fortifications.

Ten years later its environs were desolate: villages had been razed, the countryside was ravaged, crops had been devastated and destroyed. Raymond desperately needed to augment his revenues and re-people his domains. Immediately on his accession he decided to found a new town a few kilometres west of Saint-Marcel-Campes, on the 70-metre-high-hill of Mordagne which dominates the surrounding lands and the valley of the Cérou.

He intended this bastion to defend a vast territory, stretching far across the Ségala plateau. Raymond was justifiably anxious. Though Simon de Montfort was dead, his son Amaury was still marauding throughout the count's realms and the Capetian monarchy in the north still threatened his autonomy. In building a new town to guard against these threats, Count Raymond VII of Toulouse created the first French bastide.

Raymond named his new town Cordoue, after the Spanish city of Córdoba. Today Cordes presents itself as 'the city in the sky'. The limbs of every visitor are likely to be taxed by the slopes of the defensive site Count Raymond chose, and the particularly steep steps down to the gateway known as the *porte du Planol* are known as the 'pater noster', since their number matches the words of the Lord's Prayer in Latin.

From the beginning Cordes was surrounded by a double row of fortifications, pierced by defensive gates. Still standing from the first ring of walls are the so-called *porte des Ormeaux* and the *portail peint*. From the second remain the *porte de la Jane* and the *porte du Planol*. They surround an ensemble which is bisected by the Grand'rue, which aimed at being straight but veers a little because of the lie of the land. Other streets run off at right angles to it.

Today Cordes is virtually traffic-free, save for the vehicles owned by its inhabitants and in particular those of the artist community which has perfectly restored the bastide. From the west visitors enter by way of the powerful *porte de la Jane*, with its semicircular towers, immediately passing through the *porte des Ormeaux* of the inner city wall, again defended by two massive towers. You can make out that once it also boasted a portcullis and was closed by a huge wooden door.

As Count Raymond VII intended, Cordes prospered. Outside the bastide the devastated countryside was replanted with linen and hemp. In spite of the Black Death, throughout the Middle Ages Cordes never seriously declined. Cloth merchants, weavers and dyers, as well as craftsmen creating leather goods, built at the centre of the bastide a group of medieval houses out of the local sandstone, as beautiful as any in the south-west of France. Arcaded, their walls pierced with ogival windows, some of them are enhanced with sculpture. The elegant house of the falconer (the *maison du Grand Fauconnier*) derives its name from carved birds which once decorated its façade. The house of the hunter (the *maison du Grand Veneur*) still retains its frieze of sculpted animals and hunters above the Gothic windows of the third storey. At the centre of the frieze are carved two strange heads, said to represent Count Raymond VII de Toulouse and his countess.

From a corner of the house of the huntsman (the *maison du Grand Ecuyer*) juts the carved head of a horse, while other sculptures on this building depict mythological beasts, a man playing bagpipes and a woman munching an apple. Another superb medieval house is the *maison Fontpeyrouse*, with a courtyard and two storeys of wooden galleries.

At the heart of Cordes is its market place, with the market hall which became a central feature of every subsequent bastide. The original market square of Cordes soon proved insufficient for the merchants attracted here and was enlarged. The monumental hall, which rises on twenty-four octagonal stone pillars, was built in 1353, five years after the outbreak of the Black Death. This lovely building signals the speedy return to prosperity of the town.

Close by is the parish church. Significantly, in this defensive town, it was dedicated to the pious warrior Saint Michael. From its original thirteenth-century foundation it retains only the apse and two side chapels in the choir. The rest dates mostly from the fourteenth century, though the nave dates from the fifteenth century and the organ came from Notre-Dame-de-Paris only in 1840. Even this house of God bears witness to the defensive needs of the turbulent era in which it was founded. Its belfry is connected to a watchtower which rises at the highest point of the bastide. The arrangement was entirely practical. At the approach of an enemy, the lookout would warn the clergy, who would alert the citizens to the danger by ringing the church bells.

Further evidence of the dangers of the thirteenth and fourteenth centuries is the barbican at Cordes, a powerful tower set in the eastern ramparts of the bastide. Evidently these defensive arrangements failed to satisfy the inhabitants, for in successive centuries they encircled Cordes with two more walls, of which vestiges still remain including the *porte de l'Horloge* (the clock was in fact added only in the seventeenth century).

But where did the men and women come from to build this bastide? How were they lured here? Count Raymond VII of Toulouse wished not only to construct a fortified new town with a market square and a parish church. He also needed to people his new foundation with citizens loyal to himself and his successors. He attracted them by offering hitherto unparalleled rights. By a charter dated 4 November 1222, which still exists, Raymond exempted anyone who wished to make a home in Cordes from any annual service, from payments, from slavery. They were to be ruled by consuls elected by themselves. By the end of the century some 6000 had been beguiled by these terms to live here.

When the treaty of Meaux brought the Albigensian crusade to an end in 1229, Cordes nominally came under the sovereignty of the kings of France. In 1283, King Philippe III the Bold, considering that the charter granted by Raymond VII was now obsolete, renewed the rights of the citizens with a new one. But in spite of Raymond VII's apparent return to Catholicism, the bastide remained Cathar until the fourteenth century, determinedly resisting the assaults of the inquisitors. On the south side of the market place is a well, 113 metres deep. A plaque beside it declares that the nearby Gothic cross, fashioned out of iron, commemorates three inquisitors sent here by the bishop of Albi to seek out heretics and promptly drowned in the well by the citizens of the bastide.

One of the most ferocious persecutors of Cathars, Bishop Bernard de Castanet, finally cleansed Cordes of the heresy at the beginning of the fourteenth century. On 19 June, 1321 the consuls and people of the bastide gathered in the market square and, in the presence of preaching friars and inquisitors, begged pardon for their offences. They were absolved.

Catharism had survived for almost a century in the shelter of Raymond VII's bastide. In the meantime the Catholics had not been slow to emulate the heretics in building similar defensive towns to secure their hold on the Languedoc. In particular Amaury de Montfort created one, named Montfort, a few kilometres due west of Albi. (In the fourteenth century it passed into the hands of the Lévis family, changing its name to Labastide-de-Lévis, by which it is still known.) In 1269, Philippe de Montfort, the son of Simon's brother Guy, who was by that time lord of the former Cathar stronghold of Castres, created a bastide to which he accorded so many rights that it named itself Free City – Villa-Franca. It sits today on the D99 south-east of Albi, under its present name Villefranche-d'Albigeois. Eight years later Philippe de Montfort founded the bastide of Técou, which lies not far south of Labastide-de-Lévis.

These Catholic bastides are surpassed in magnificence by those foun-ded by Louis IX himself. The first was Aigues-Mortes. Possessing no Mediterranean port, in 1246 Louis bought land on the Rhône delta from the abbey of Psalmodi and there built on the coast a fortified city. Its walls today rise from flat salt-marshes sprinkled with dead lagoons (the *aquae mortuae* from which the bastide takes its name). An extremely generous charter granted by Louis attracted independent citizens. He built the 30 metre-high *tour de Constance*, a circular keep overlooking a vast stretch of countryside, in part desolate, in part supporting vineyards.

On 28 August, 1248, Louis set sail from here for Egypt on the Seventh Crusade, after days of feasting and jousts. The remnants of his fleet returned empty-handed, the heathen still dominant in the Holy Land. Twenty years later the king returned to Aigues-Mortes, but this time there were no feasts: he anxiously brooded in his tent. Only half as many crusaders as before set sail with him on his last crusade. The plague ravaged his camp at Tunis, and on 25 August, 1270, Louis himself succumbed. The pope canonized him in 1297.

Two years later his son, Philippe le Hardi, engaged a Genoese engineer named Guglielmo Boccanegra to build the massive ramparts of Aigues-Mortes, which are crowned with twenty towers and pierced by mighty gateways. The north wall measures 467 metres, the south 496, while the east and west walls respectively stretch for 301 and 269 metres. Perfectly preserved, they seem to symbolize all the religious and secular aspirations of the Capetian kings. Inside, chequerboard-patterned streets converge on the place Saint-Louis.

Louis's second great bastide was created beside the ancient walled city of Carcassonne. Its tribulations throughout the thirteenth century are a mirror of that turbulent, religion-cursed era. After Simon de Montfort's death, Cathar Carcassonne, which he had successfully besieged, passed into the hands of his son Amaury, who in turn ceded suzerainty of the city to the French crown.

After his defeat by Simon de Montfort the Cathar lord of Carcassonne, Raymond 11 Trencavel, had taken refuge in Aragon. In 1240 he returned to the Languedoc in a final attempt to recover his domains. Several discontented nobles joined him in besieging the city of Carcassonne, by now superbly fortified. The siege was a failure. Only the suburbs were destroyed, some of them by their own inhabitants who set fire to their homes before fleeing.

Raymond 11 Trencavel once more took refuge in Spain. In 1247, King Louis 1x pardoned the rebel, who then loyally took part in the king's crusade against the Moors. The former heretic fought so fanatically that Louis restored to him some of his former territories in the Corbières region, and he died content.

In the same year as Raymond's pardon, Louis decided to rebuild the suburbs of Carcassonne as a new bastide, stretching along the flatlands beside the hilly site of the old city. Planned in chequerboard fashion, its streets run from a central square. Walls (today in parts represented by the boulevards which ring the city) defend the *ville basse*, as lower Carcassonne is known. Electing their own consuls, the citizens bred sheep outside the town and exported their cloth as far as Spain. Their coat of arms displayed the Lamb of God, in acknowledgement of Jesus and of the animal whose coat made them prosperous.

From the railway station runs rue Georges-Clemenceau, today traffic-free. On the left rises a thirteenth-century church, built for the Carmelites (inside which is modern stained glass depicting the prophet Elijah rising to heaven from Mount Carmel). Beyond it is the market square, nowadays known as place Carnot and centring on a flamboyant Neptune fountain created in 1770. Rue Court-Jarre leads south from the square past the municipal theatre to the impressive city walls.

The old suburbs of Carcassonne had been dedicated to Saint Michel and Saint Vincent, and Louis IX instructed the citizens of his bastide to build two churches in honour of these saints. The fortified church of Saint Michel is a splendid Gothic building, its single nave flanked with vaulted chapels. The Black Prince set fire to the *ville basse* of Carcassonne in 1355, after which the church of Saint Michel was incorporated into the city's new ramparts, its own aspect as stern as they are.

Saint Vincent is similiarly honoured with a fortified church, battle-mented, its Gothic arches rising from a Romanesque base. This is the second widest church in France (the widest is that in the bastide of Mirepoix). Its octagonal belfry rises from a square base and carries no fewer than forty-seven bells. Inside, underneath the organ, are four statues, sculpted in the fourteenth century: two represent apostles, another is of Saint Vincent, the fourth is the sole authentic portrait of Saint Louis of France.

Despite his efforts, Carcassonne remained wedded to heresy long after his death. Archdeacon Sans Morlane of Carcassonne lies buried in the transept of Saint Nazaire in the upper city, not far from the tomb of Simon de Montfort. So incensed was he that the inquisitors kept records of the religious beliefs of his parishioners that in 1283 he mounted a plot to steal the files. Three years later the consuls of Carcassonne complained to King Philippe le Bel that 'the oppressive regime of the Dominicans has resulted in mass-emigration from the royal lands, depopulation and ruin'. Philippe was less than sympathetic, and for a time withdrew the privileges of the *ville basse*, hanging Consul Elie Patrice and fifteen of his allies.

Numerous other suspect citizens of Carcassonne suffered imprisonment for their beliefs, some of them confined on a diet of bread and water, some more leniently allowed to tend a vegetable garden. Others were allowed more freedom, though forced to wear a cross and to forfeit their possessions. The last Cathar to be executed at Carcassonne was probably Guillemette Tournier. Her prison cell adjoined that of an informer, to whom she unwisely confided her deep hatred of Catholicism. She was burnt at the stake in 1325.

Lords, Monks, Knights & Pilgrims

In fourteenth-century Europe men and women were fascinated by the idea of planning new towns and cities. Around 1330, in the Tuscan city of Siena, a brilliant pupil of Giotto named Ambrogio Lorenzetti emulated his teacher's mastery of perspective to paint an aerial view of an ideal city. The painting is still intact. Although the site of this imaginary city is irregular, its internal layout is uncannily like that of a bastide, with regular parcels of houses criss-crossed by streets at right angles to each other.

Six and a half centuries later Lewis Mumford, the pioneer historian of European cities, described Lorenzetti's painting as 'the archetypal historic city of all ages, complete with its fortified citadel, its town-encircling wall, and its great portals'. For Mumford, this painting and others like it indicated 'an affectionate concern with the city as a deliberate work of art'.

What neither Lewis Mumford nor Ambrogio Lorenzetti realized was that Count Raymond VII of Toulouse got there long before they did. Over a hundred years before Lorenzetti painted his ideal city, the count was not merely imagining but building such cities. Along with Cordes, he founded four other superb bastides (as well as several minor ones). Lauzerte, today in the *département* of Tarn-et-Garonne, received its charter in 1241. In the Occitan language Lauzerte means 'lizard', and the site does resemble a 'lizard', lounging in the sum. Before Raymond VII's bastide was built, this was already a stronghold, fortified by his predecessor Raymond V.

As at Cordes, the medieval quarter perches on a hill, and today presents itself as one of the Toledos of France. Some of its fortifications have survived over the centuries, though during the wars of religion the Protestants sacked the town and massacred many of its inhabitants. The *porte de la Barbacane* (known as the 'Gandilhonne') still protects the arcaded market square and a cluster of half-timbered houses dating from the thirteenth to the fifteenth centuries.

In 1246, Count Raymond founded Puymirol, in the *département* of Lot-et-Garonne, on a prehistoric site, later inhabited by the Romans and the

Gauls, close by the ancient route between Clermont and Agen. Old documents about Puymirol, taking their cue from this route, often dub the bastide Pyrmirol Clermontoise. Its fairs dated back to the early twelfth century. Raymond fortified it, and although in the early sixteenth century King Louis XIII ordered its 800-metre-long walls to be demolished, traces of them can still be seen, as you wind your way to the hilltop site. A long, straight street now leads to the arcaded market square, with its well, its stone houses and a market hall for selling corn. Beyond it rises the Romanesque tower of a church once dedicated to Saint-Sernin (which predates the bastide and sat alone at an important crossroads), its thirteenth-century porch decorated with seven Gothic arches and set amidst the irregular white stones of the original building.

Although this parish church (now dedicated to Notre-Dame-du-Grand-Castel) was partly rebuilt in the seventeenth century, its restored belfry rises from a thirteenth-century base. The bastide's site is also important, dominating from its long plateau the surrounding countryside. Count Raymond, who dubbed it the 'grande castrum', relied on Puymirol to protect the western limit of his territory.

As for its charter, some of the requirements seem particularly severe. A lawyer who made a mistake was to have his right hand chopped off. Adulterers were to parade naked through the streets, tied together, before being exposed in the pillory. Anyone who killed a person was to be buried underneath the victim. Wine merchants were required to swear that they had not added water to their goods.

Next Count Raymond founded Montesquieu-Volvestre (in the *département* of Haute-Garonne), set both picturesquely and strategically beside a bend of the River Arize. He gave it a charter in the same year as he founded Puymirol. Eight years previously Raymond had bought a twelfth-century château nearby this new foundation. Along with medieval houses, some of them half-timbered, and a fourteenth-century château, his bastide has retained its arcaded central square, with a solid, fourteenth century market hall whose wooden beams are roofed with pantiles. The church best displays the defensive strength of Montesquieu-Volvestre. Dating from the fourteenth to the sixteenth centuries and built of brick, it displays crenellations, a pepperpot tower on either side of its rose window and a massive polygonal tower (with a modern clock oddly set in its second storey). The rose window in its façade is the sole opening, for the intention of those who built the church was to make it impregnable in time of war. The porch is Renaissance in style, with fluted Corinthian columns. Inside is a single nave, flanked by side chapels.

The old quarters of Raymond's last bastide, Lisle-sur-Tarn, are also brick-built, some of the houses also half-timbered. Here the fortress of Montaigut, four kilometres north-west, had been destroyed on the orders of the French monarchy in 1229 (save for its chapel). Count Raymond founded Lisle-sur-Tarn a year before his death, on a plot of land washed by the River Tarn and two streams, the Rabisteau and the Vignal. The Gothic church of Notre-Dame-de-la-Jonquière, built of brick and in part fortified, has a thirteenth-century Romanesque tower, 40 metres high, pierced with twin windows, decorated with gargoyles and topped with an octagonal spire. Though much of the church was rebuilt from the fourteenth to the sixteenth centuries, its Romanesque porch remains as it was in the thirteenth. Inside is a huge eighteenth-century reredos.

As with all Raymond's bastides, the central square is arcaded. This is the largest such square in south-west France, and from it run streets set out at right angles to each other. In some of the narrow passages the first-floor levels of the houses on either side are joined by covered passageways, known as 'pontets', so that the occupants could cross over each other's houses without having to go out of doors. And as with all defensive towns, Lisle-sur-Tarn's citizens dug a well, this one in the market square.

Yet of all these new towns Cordes remains the most astonishingly original creation. Its geometrical chequerboard pattern; its defensive ramparts; its market square; its civic charter – this combination had never been seen in France until Raymond VII of Toulouse founded the bastide. It was to set the pattern for some 600 new towns, created in south-west France in little more than 150 years.

Nothing happens *de novo*. Historians of the bastides point out that the creation of these new cities was no isolated phenomenon in south-west France. Count Raymond could draw on three distinct urban developments which preceded his undertaking: hospices, *sauvetés*, and *castelnaux*.

Hospices evolved as the result of a pilgrimage, the most popular in western Christendom. At the height of its medieval popularity some 500,000 pilgrims annually arrived at the shrine of Saint James the Great in Santiago de Compostela. Count Raymond of Toulouse himself made the pilgrimage in 1232, generously bequeathing lands worth twenty livres a year to the monks of Roncesvalles in gratitude for the welcome they had shown him.

At times the route proved dangerous. Aimery Picaud, a Cluniac monk of Parthenay-le-Vieux who wrote a medieval guide to the pilgrimage, observed that the people of Navarre 'would murder a pilgrim for a sou'. Parts of the pilgrimage route in Spain, he reported, were infested with brigands. In consequence, the Knights Templars, an order founded around 1120 to protect pilgrims to the Holy Land from attacks by bands of Muslims, soon began escorting pilgrims to Santiago de Compostela.

Throughout France and Spain they built hospices along the pilgrimage routes. Men and women were needed to provide these hospices with goods, to till the fields, to build and repair, indeed to bury the dead (for many pilgrims succumbed without ever reaching their destination). Such people were readily available. Some of them were outcasts of society, looking for a new life: runaway serfs, brigands looking for security, men and women fleeing from justice. Others simply had no work, for the twelfth and thirteenth centuries witnessed a remarkable expansion of Europe's population.

Thus the countryside of the bastides is speckled with a remarkable earlier pattern of settlement, embryonic bastides so to speak. No one seeking out bastides should neglect them. An example is Arfons in the Tarn, an ancient village at the western extremity of the Montagne-Noire which clusters around the former commandery of the Knights Hospitallers. Along with its Romanesque church, Sarrazac in the Lot retains vestiges of the Templars' château and the hospice they built for pilgrims to Rocamadour and to the shrine of Saint James in Spain. A second example is Figeac in the same *département*, which also lies on an important pilgrimage route to Santiago de Compostela. Figeac grew around an abbey founded in 838 which in 1085 amalgamated with the mother house of Cluny. Philippe le Bel granted its citizens a charter and the right to mint their own money: the medieval *hôtel de monnaie* still stands. The abbey granted them the right to elected their own consuls, again a precursor of the rights of the citizens of the bastides. Figeac even boasted a thirteenth-century corn market until 1888, when it was demolished.

Although the Knights Templars fell out of favour with the temporal authorities of France and were eventually abolished, their foundations survived them. Their fall from grace was probably undeserved. In the fourteenth century, so great was the wealth and power of the Templars that King Philippe le Bel grew extremely alarmed. He also wished to appropriate their lands and wealth. In 1312, Philippe persuaded Pope Clement V that the Templars were both immoral and heretical. The order was suppressed, and Jacques de Molay, Grand Master of the Knights Templar, was burned at the stake in 1314.

Their role and many of their hospices were taken over by the Knights Hospitallers. Founded in 1070, they too protected pilgrims to the Holy Land. When Jerusalem fell in 1290, these knights moved first to Cyprus and then became the lords of Rhodes. The Turks drove them out and, after settling again in Cyprus and then in Sicily, they finally made their base at Malta, hence their alternative name, Knights of Malta, and the Maltese cross which henceforth invariably appeared in their insignia.

Crusaders who had benefited from their protection bestowed lands on the Templars and the Hospitallers. And as is implied by the very name Hospitaller (from the old French *hospitalier*, which in turn derives from the Latin *hospes* or guest), alongside their commanderies they also built hospices to shelter pilgrims overnight.

These new towns and villages were often granted charters setting out their citizens' rights and duties. In the case of the Knights Templars, their dependencies included the town of Mazères-sur-Salat in the Haute-Garonne which has two charters, one of 1228, the other of 1291. Almost adjacent is the fortified town of Montsaunès, where you can still see the remains of a Templar commandery, where the twelfth-century church is built of brick, and where the citizens have enjoyed a charter of privileges since 1288.

As for the Hospitallers, Caignac for instance, which lies south-east of Toulouse, came into their possession in 1136. The citizens began to elect their own consuls in 1239 and its franchises were renewed in a new charter of 1299. A little nearer Toulouse is the fortified town of Fonsorbes, with its twelfth-century Gothic church. Fonsorbes belonged to the Hospitallers from the eleventh century, and received its charter in 1209.

Bastides eventually performed the same service to pilgrims as these earlier foundations. By the end of the thirteenth century pilgrims to Santiago de Compostela would find even greater security in the new towns. North of Bordeaux, for instance, pilgrims were particularly well cared for in this way before the end of the thirteenth century.

The first bastide they would reach was Libourne, whose name derives from the English seneschal Roger of Leyburn, founder of the bastide in 1268. Libourne commands the strategic confluence of the Dordogne and the Isle. The most characteristic remnants of its days as a bastide are the typical chequerboard layout and a market place with covered arcades under the houses typical of many bastides. Here they surround an elaborate eighteenth-century fountain, and here too rises the sixteenth-century Gothic town hall, surrounded by contemporary houses. Libourne was fortified in the early fourteenth century. Unfortunately, in the nineteenth its battlements were destroyed, save for the two towers of the *porte du Grand Port* and a few vestiges that can be seen in the rue des Murs.

In 1476 the mayor of Libourne, Jean Decazes, had a copy made of its charter of 1392. The manucript still exists, bound in sheepskin which still retains its fleece. Inside is depicted the crucifixion. The preface runs: 'This is the book of the community of the city of Libourne, in which are all the manners and forms of of promises which the king of France and duke of Guyenne and each of his nominated seneschals must make, and also the duties of the community.'

Libourne's church, dedicated to Saint John, was built in the twelfth century and transformed in the fourteenth and fifteenth. Its pride is a thorn from the crown of thorns which the crucified Jesus was forced to wear. The chapel of Condat in the same bastide boasts a miracle working statue of Mary and the Infant Jesus, carved out of oak in the sixteenth century.

Further south the pilgrims would reach the bastides of Blasimon and Sauveterre-de-Guyenne. Blasimon is surrounded by ancient windmills, a sign of the prosperity a bastide could bring to the countryside. The finest of these is fortified, the *moulin de Labarthe*, which was built in the turbulent fourteenth century. This bastide was founded by Benedictine monks, and their ruined abbey of Saint-Maurice still stands here, as does the abbey church; its Romanesque church is in much better condition, with an exceptionally fine sculpted porch, the carvings repesenting the vices and virtues as well as hunting scenes. Blasimon's central square is picturesquely arcaded.

A Romanesque church which once belonged to the Knights Templars blesses the hamlet of Le Puch, between Blasimon and the bastide of Sauveterre-de-Guyenne. Edward 1 of England founded Sauveterre-de-Guyenne in 1281, in a spot where a Benedictine priory had stood since the ninth century and on land which he bought from the local seigneur, Jordan de Puch. Although its walls were demolished in 1838, its four Gothic gates still survive (the finest the *porte Saubotte*), as well as medieval houses, and a medieval fountain and wash house. The corn market is still arcaded, some arches round, others pointed, providing a covered way under the houses; and though the parish church was restored in the nineteenth century, it retains its polygonal Gothic choir.

Soon the pilgrims would arrive at the majestic ruins of the Benedictine abbey of La Sauve-Majeure, founded by Saint Gérard in the forest of Sylva-Major in 1079. The Romanesque church and abbey are today in ruins. Saint Gérard's mortal remains lie in the local parish church of Saint-Pierre. Frescoed on its apse is a mythical portrait of Saint James the Great, who is also sculpted inside the parish church as well as on a romanesque capital of the ruined abbey.

Three kilometres further towards Bordeaux, the pilgrims could seek shelter in another bastide. Founded in the early fourteenth century by Amaury de Créon, a seneschal of the king of England, Créon has a fifteenth-century Gothic church with a seventeenth-century belfry, streets at right angles to each other and a market square (the place de la Prévôté) surrounded by arcades.

Leaving Bordeaux, medieval pilgrims to Santiago de Compostela next found a resting place at Gradignan in the hospice of Cayac which was founded in the twelfth century by the Knights Hospitallers.

In addition to the shelter provided by villages under the rule of the Templars and the Hospitallers, since the mid-eleventh century some churches, and especially powerful abbeys had been founding other settlements known as *sauvetés*, a good number of them along the same pilgrimage route to Santiago de Compostela. Many aspects of these new settlements also laid down a pattern for the bastides. Usually grouped around a great church or a monastery, they offered protection to refugees from justice, to those dispossessed of their land and to intrepid persons who had no desire to acknowledge a feudal lord.

Pre-eminent in founding *sauvetés* were the abbeys of Conques, Sauve-Majeure and Sainte-Croix at Bordeaux. Their religious origin was recognized in the crosses which stood at the boundaries of each *sauveté*. You can still see the bases of five of these medieval crosses at Mimizan, south-east of Bordeaux (where the ruins of its Benedictine abbey include a superbly sculpted porch depicting Jesus and his apostles, the wise and foolish virgins, and the signs of the zodiac).

Today their existence is equally easily recognized in towns and villages whose names include the words Sauvetat or Salvetat. Two such still exist in the *département* of Haute-Garonne. La Salvetat-Lauragais has a sixteenth century Gothic church, sculpted with lovely friezes, and a château with a keep. La Salvetat-Saint-Gilles in the same *département* is where the parliament of Toulouse took refuge during the plague of 1581. Not all such new villages and towns had this nomenclature, however: just south of Albi is Carlus, a *sauveté* created by the cathedral chapter of Saint Cécile.

Cistercian monks were required by the rules of their order to till their own fields, a duty which many found burdensome. Such monks needed lay persons to serve their foundations, sometimes ordaining them in one of the lesser orders of the church, so as not to break the monastic rule. Few lay people found this a satisfactory way of life. To attract sufficient farming families, the monks were obliged to offer them plots of land to cultivate, space to build a house and numerous privileges, these last specifically set out in charters.

So, for example, in the *département* of Lot-et-Garonne the inhabitants of La Sauvetat-de-Savères, which has a twelfth-century church and lies in the valley of the Séoune, received its charter in 1205. In the eleventh century the monks of Condom created a *sauveté* in the *département* of Gers which is still simply called La Sauvetat, a picturesque village of narrow streets, ancient fountains, windmills and little squares which has also preserved some of its fortifications. Its charter of rights and duties dates from 1271. Another former *sauveté* is Marignac-Laspeyres, on the route to Santiago de Compostela which runs through the Haute-Garonne, which was founded in the twelfth century and received its charter in 1274.

For the sake of collective security, the homes of these sauvetés were sometimes built close together, running off at right angles from the main street and thus forming a model which was adopted in many later bastides. In the *département* of Gers, Nogaro was so designed, founded in 1060 by Saint Austinde, archbishop of Auch, who also built the Romanesque church which still stands there.

After the foundations of the Knights Templars and Knights Hospital-lers, and alongside the *sauvetés* of the eleventh century, the third precursor of French bastides is the type of town which often took the name Castelnau (from the Latin *castrum* camp). Usually built on hills dominating the sur-rounding countryside, these new towns were generally surrounded by for-midable walls. Sometimes, to afford further protection to the inhabitants, they clustered around châteaux.

In the Aveyron, both Castelnau-Pégayrols and Castelnau-de-Mandailles are still protected by the remains of fortifications and fortresses. Castelnau-d'Anglès in the *département* of Gers once belonged to the Knights of Malta. On a bailey there rises the château of Lasséran. Castelnau-sur-l'Auvignon in the same *département*, on a route to Santiago de Compostela, also has a fortress, this one however ruined, with a huge round tower. Castelnau-d'Auzun has a thirteenth-century château. Only the tower remains of the former château of Castelnau-Barbarens, but the town has retained one of the medieval gates from its ramparts. As with the foundations of the Templars and the Hospitallers, as with the *sauvetés*, many of these new towns were granted franchises and charters. Hilltop Castelnau-d'Estretefonds in Haute-Garonne received its charter in 1131. At Castelnau-Montratier in the département of the Lot you can still see the consuls' house as well as the arcaded square in which the citizens exercised their right to hold a weekly market.

New towns were thus being built in south west France a century or more before Raymond VII of Toulouse founded Cordes, towns moreover which often afforded special privileges to attract sturdily independent inhabitants. In these places, some of the techniques of attracting citizens to colonize a new town were developed before anyone began building bas-tides. Charters, fortified sites, market squares surrounded by cool arcades and sometimes enclosing a market hall, and finally chequerboard patterns of urban design were deployed in Templar and Hospitaller foundations, in *sauvetés* and in the *castelnaux*.

Although these four elements – the charter, the chequerboard lay-out of the town, the fortifications and the central market place – generally speedily identify a genuine bastide, there are some spots where it is impossible to be certain, either because the charter has disappeared or there is no historical record of it, or else because in later centuries parts of the original foundation have been razed. Montpezat-de-Quercy in the *département* of Tarn-et-Garonne is a good example of this problem. Situated on a defensive hill once inhabited by the Gauls, it had became a seat of the Montpezat family by the eleventh century. Their château was demolished in 1793. In between the English had pillaged the town during the Hundred Years War.

Yet Montpezat-de-Quercy retains some of its fortifications, and an abso-lutely typical bastide corn market, save for the fact that it is triangular, inevitably in view of the site. In the middle is a well. Stone and half-timbered houses, with different styles of arcading, surround the square. Today the square is called the place de la Résistance, and a plaque on one wall is dedicated to the memory of Marie-Antoinette Ocival, who was arrested on 2 May 1944 and deported to Ravensbruck concentration camp. She died in Hamburg on 15 June, 1945.

Montpezat-de-Quercy received its charter of privileges from the count of Toulouse in 1257. Today it is worth visiting if only for the splendid collegiate church of Saint Martin of Tours, which Cardinal Pierre des Prés built in 1334. The church stands outside the walls of the bastide, reached by walking downhill along rue du Château. Its simple fortress tower has a rose window, and through the Gothic porch you enter a fine example of a French southern Gothic church. The bosses of its ogival valting are carved with the cardinal's coat of arms. He lies in a tomb on the right of the entrance to the choir, his sculpted effigy resting its feet on a little lion. On the left of the apse is a tomb with the effigy of his nephew, Bishop Jean des Prés of Castres.

The glory of the church is a sixteenth-century Flemish tapestry, which stretches around the whole choir above the carved canons' stalls. This was the gift of Jean IV des Prés, bishop of Montauban, and the family coat of arms, with the addition of a mitre and crozier, is woven into the tapestry. Like an elaborate strip cartoon, a sequence of woven illustrations depicts the life of the patron of the church, beginning with Saint Martin on a superb white charger slicing his cloak in two for a beggar (who happens not to be naked, so that it is hard to know why he needs half of the saint's cloak) and ending with his death, a horrid demon vainly attempting to steal his soul.

Above each scene, in exceedingly quaint French, a poem recounts what is happening. Martin, for instance, lies asleep in a four-poster bed (on one of whose posts there happens to be painted the coat of arms of Jean VI des Prés), and has a dream in which God appears in the sky, along with angels who tell him that in truth he gave his cloak to the Almighty himself. The rhyme runs:

> Luy reposant comme transy
> Dieu se appparut anv onné
> de Angels auquel disait ainsy:
> Martin ce manteau m'a donné.

To my mind the most humorous scene depicts Martin celebrating Mass, his congregation two chattering women. Unbeknown to them, the devil is taking down their gossip.

Faced with such riches, one might almost miss the fourteenth-century carved Madonna in this church, her hair curly and red, her infant son's head unfortunately knocked off. The church stands in the place des Martyrs, where on 2 May 1944 the Nazis shot three members of the Resistance named Félix Depech, Jean Costes and Reinl Bathe.

The question to be addressed is whether the origins of Montpezat-de-Quercy predate the era of the bastides. Even if they do, however, that is no reason to deny the bastide status. All three medieval precursors, hospices, *sauvetés, castelnaux*, tended to evolve into bastides, and in many cases we can trace the process. In the *département* of Haute-Garonne are two which began life as commanderies of the Knights Hospitallers. They founded and fortified Montastruc-la-Conseillière, which was transformed into a bastide in 1242, while their town of Saint-Sulpice-sur-Lèze also became a bastide, transformed in 1257 on the order of Alphonse de Poitiers, count of Toulouse. Its arcaded central square is still intact, with half-timbered houses rising from wooden pillars. The Hospitallers' church was rebuilt between 1450 and 1458 and now constitutes a splendid example of Languedocian Gothic architecture, its octagonal belfry topped with a brick, crocketed spire.

Again, Montfaucon, perched on a hill in the Lot, along with the church of Saint-Vézian and the little community around it, had belonged first to the Templars and then to the Hospitallers a century before the officers of Edward II of England transformed the town into a bastide. And the very name of Labastide-du-Temple (in the Tarn-et-Garonne) derives from precisely such a transformation.

La Sauvetat-du-Dropt in the Lot-et-Garonne is a perfect example of a *sauveté* which transformed itself into a bastide in the thirteenth century. This was one of the last places in Aquitaine to be held by the English during the

Hundred Years War. Much ravaged during the wars of religion, La Sauvetat-du-Dropt nevertheless retains thirteenth-century houses in its old quarter, vestiges of its ramparts, and a fourteen-arched, thirteenth-century bridge spanning the River Dropt. In the Grand'rue is a superb Renaissance house. An inscription on the Romanesque parish church of Saint Gervais, which was restored in the sixteenth century, reveals that the building was damaged by a cyclone in 1242.

Just as the etymology of Labastide-du Temple indicates a Templars' hospice transformed into a bastide, sometimes you can read in a name the development of a *sauveté* into a bastide. Sauveterre-de-Rouergue in the Avey-ron, one of France's most exquisite villages, is a bastide founded in 1281 by Guillaume, seneschal of Vienne and Mâcon, on behalf of the king of France. *Sauveterre*, obviously a cognate of *sauveté*, signifies free land. The bastide guards the rivers Lieux and Lézert. Of its fortifications remain two gates, Saint-Christophe and Saint-Vital. The arcaded central square is huge, measuring 60 by 40 metres, houses jut out over covered walkways, the lay-out is geometrical. A thirteenth-century keep, the *tour de Castelnau*, has survived.

The fourteenth-century collegiate church of Sauveterre-de-Rouerge has a tower which matches this keep in defensive fearsomeness and turns out to have been the keep of the bastide's former fortress. An air of less warlike homeliness is exuded by half-timbered houses, some of their façades entranc-ingly sculpted, some of their doors with ogival vaulting. The old windmills scarcely indicate the former prosperity of this bastide (which declined in the nineteenth century when the railway passed it by). In past times it was peopled by cobblers and by those who made their nails, by weavers and by rope makers, as well as by farmers and millers.

Directly west of Sauveterre-de-Rouergue lies another bastide whose name indicates that it developed from a *sauveté*. Dominating no fewer than four rivers (the Viaur, the Liort, the Jaoul and the Lézert), La Salvetat-Peyralès began life as a dependency of Rodez cathedral. It was transformed into a bastide in the thirteenth century, and thenceforth administered by elected *jurats*.

Count Raymond VII of Toulouse himself was responsible for founding two *castelnaux* which later became bastides. Both lie in the present-day *département* of the Tarn. In 1235, Castelnau-de-Lévis was created on his orders by Sicard I d'Alaman, as a refuge for those whose neighbouring villages had been ruined by Simon de Montfort. The old town rises on a hill, its watchtower still partly intact, its château and walls in ruins, its fortified thirteenth century church well worth a visit. The citizens received their charter in 1256. Castelnau-de-Montmiral is another hilltop bastide, with an arcaded market square (restored in 1986) and a fifteenth-century Gothic church. Once protected by six gates, it has preserved only one, the *porte des Garrics*.

A yet finer bastide originating as a *castelnau* is Castelnau-Montratier in the Lot. Situated south of Cahors, on a height which dominates to the north the River Barguelonne and to the south the River Lutte, it began life as Castelnau-de-Vaux. During the Albigensian crusade its Cathar lord seized Bauduin, brother of the count of Toulouse, and delivered his prisoner to the count of Foix, who had Bauduin hanged. In reprisal, Simon de Montfort burned Castelnau-de-Vaux and its château to the ground. On the site of this former château Ratier de Castelnau rebuilt the *castelnau* as a bastide around 1350, and the present name Castelnau-Montratier derives in part from his.

Its central square — today shaded by limes and chestnut trees — is triangular, bordered with arcades. Among the medieval houses of the bastide is the fifteenth-century house of the consuls. Three ancient windmills on the route to Cahors testify to the prosperity of this bastide.

Of the three types of precursor of the bastides, settlements created to protect pilgrims to Santiago de Compostela probably had the strongest influence. As with the Templars' and Hospitallers' foundations, we find *sauvetés* on the pilgrimage route transformed into classic bastides. In the

Aveyron stands the great Benedictine abbey of Conques, itself a centre of pilgrimage since one of its monks in the ninth century managed to steal from the monks of Agen the remains of Saint Foy, a young Christian girl martyred in the fourth century. Around 1050, these Benedictines founded a priory dedicated to her at Sainte-Foy-de-Peyrolières, south-west of Toulouse and on a major route to Santiago de Compostela. By 1255, when Count Alphonse II of Toulouse and the abbot of Conques came to an agreement to develop Sainte-Foy-de-Peyrolières as a bastide, the settlement that had grown up around the priory had already received its charter.

Further south along the pilgrimage route, another Benedictine monastery flourished at Larreaule, and here still stands the monks' former abbey church, originally Romanesque as remains its apse. In the thirteenth century these Benedictines transformed Larreaule into a bastide, its surviving windmill a testimony to its former prosperity. Elsewhere other religious orders did the same for the same reasons. South-east of Tarbes, for instance, on another pilgrimage route to Spain, Cistercian monks built the bastide of Réjeaumont in 1285.

On the major route from Paris to Santiago de Compostela lies another superb bastide which developed out of a Benedictine foundation. Even before the Benedictines came, prehistoric people had lived at Sorde-l'Abbaye, leaving us their grotto of the Grand Pastou at the foot of the cliff. The Romans built a villa on the site, which looks down on to the River Oloron. The former abbot's house also overlooks a spring discovered by the Romans, who relished the spot as a mini-spa. If you step down into the three-aisled interior of the fortified abbey church you discover that its choir incorporates a Gallo-Roman mosaic, depicting animals and birds eerily staring at each other, and a dog chasing a rabbit.

Save for the abbey church, little remains of the monastic buildings, which were last restored in the seventeenth century. Built out of bands of brick and stone, the former abbey church is massively buttressed. As a protection against invaders, its lower parts boast scarcely a single window. Yet its decor proclaims the Christian gospel. Over the porch are twelfth-century Romanesque carvings, depicting Jesus in majesty, with five foolish virgins awaiting their Lord's return with unlit lamps while five wise ones wait with their lamps alight. Among these mutilated carvings you can just make out the bull, symbol of the evangelist Saint Mark, and the beak of an eagle which is the symbol of Saint John.

In 1290 the abbot of Sorde-l'Abbaye made an agreement with King Philippe IV of France to transform the village that had grown around his abbey into a bastide. These days its late thirteenth-century ramparts are covered in ivy, with an occasional door let into them as well as the original arches. The central square, as sleepy as can be, is surrounded by arcaded houses dating from the fifteenth to the eighteenth centuries.

Pilgrims brought wealth to the monasteries, whether in outright gifts, in offerings made at their shrines, or in paying for food and lodgings. To attract some of the thousands on their way to Santiago de Compostela was especially profitable. Throughout France and Spain, Cluniac monks particularly fostered this pilgrimage. They too founded new towns, with hospices for the pilgrims, and needed to attract citizens to live in them. In two of the new towns the Cluniacs created in Spain, the name itself, Villafranca, proclaimed the free status of the citizens.

Villafranca del Bierzo in Castile grew up around the collegiate church of Santa María del Cluniaco, whose monks in 1220 were granted a tenth of the tolls paid by pilgrims who passed through the town. And Villafranca Montes d'Oca on the same pilgrimage route (with a hospice dedicated to Saint Antony Abbot) was even peopled by French men and women. Like the bastides, these free towns were granted charters offering their citizens special privileges.

Not surprisingly, a good number of their bastide counterparts in France dubbed themselves Villefranche or something similar. One of them nestles in the *département* of the Lot, in the valley of the Cère, under the name Bretenoux; but when the lord of Castelnau founded this bastide in 1277 he called it Villafranca, in the Spanish fashion.

Just south of Bayonne a *sauveté* founded in the eleventh century by the bishop of that city went so far in the next century as to change its name from Saint-Martin-de-Basters to Villefranque. We have already come across Philippe de Toulouse's foundation Villefranche d'Albigeois. Not far from the Spanish border, in the *département* of Pyrénées-Orientales, is Villefranche-de-Conflent, which was founded in 1092 by Count Guifred de Cerdagne. Fortified in the seventeenth century and again in 1783, it has otherwise scarcely changed since the Middle Ages. Romanesque and Gothic houses line its narrow, shady streets. The church of Saint-Jacques, patron saint of Santiago de Compostela, is twelfth-century Romanesque. Shortly after its foundation this unpretentious spot was granted franchises exempting its citizens from taxes and conferring on them the right to hold their own tribunal.

In the *département* of Gers a little bastide which overlooks the wooded slopes of the valley of the Gimont is named simply Villefranche. It grew up around a fortress built by the count of Astarac, who in 1297 gave the villagers a charter of privileges and rights. Villefranche-de-Lauragais is another such bastide, noted today for its cassoulets but equally notable for its thirteenth- and fourteenth-century Gothic church, with a fine belfry wall. Founded around 1270, it received its charter of privileges ten years later. Villefranche-de-Panat is a third, set beside its lake in the wooded plateau of the Lévezou between Rodez and Millau and nowadays a centre of tourism. The bastide took its present name only in 1297, when Count Pierre de Panat gave it its charter.

Two bastides in the Dordogne also took the name Villefranche. Villefranche-de-Lonchat lies just inside the western boundary of the *département*, overlooking its vineyards from a rocky crest. This is a rare example of a bastide without a church, though the inhabitants are served by the superb Gothic church built in the fourteenth and fifteenth centuries just outside the town. They received their charter of privileges in 1286.

The second Dordogne bastide specifically described as a free city is one of the loveliest in the *département*. Despite the lie of the land (the bastide overlooks the Lémance and is set in a circle of wooded hills) as well as pillaging and rebuilding over the centuries, Villefranche-du-Périgord retains the grid pattern of its streets. One of its towers is known as the *tour des Consuls*, in memory of its former elected rulers. The ancient corn measures can still be seen in the market square, where the beautifully constructed wooden roof of the market hall rises on massive stone pillars, while the surrounding stone houses are arcaded. Here too is a fountain which has served Villefranche-du-Périgord probably since the bastide was founded in 1260. The nearby church, a nineteenth-century building, is a trifle fearsome and perhaps not very elegant. More interesting is another religious building which became the home of the White Penitents (an order designed for humble folk drawn to the religious life, as opposed to the Blue Penitents, which catered for similarly minded nobility). The statues on the building were mutilated during the Revolution, but over the lintel you can still read the inscription *Si Deus pro nobis quis contra nos* ('If God be for us, who can be against us?').

If Villefranche-du-Périgord is charming, undoubtedly the most impressive of this group of bastides is Villefranche-de-Rouergue. Alphonse de Poitiers, the brother of Louis IX, founded it in 1252 on a site that was at once breathtakingly beautiful and also ideally suited to promote trade and prosperity. At the confluence of the rivers Aveyron and Alzou, where the former divides the chalk upland of Ségala from that of Villeneuve, and surrounded by rich, cultivable lands, the bastide lies where the Roman road from Montauban to Montpellier crossed the Roman road from Rodez to Cahors.

On the left bank of the Aveyron the counts of Toulouse had already founded a village known as La Peyrade. Before that time the Gauls had mined the region for copper, tin and silver. But Alphonse de Poitiers' chief impulse in founding Villefranche-de-Rouergue was to respond to a revolt in 1249 by the bastide of Najac which threatened his authority in the whole of the Rouergue (the traditional name of the territory which became the *département* of the Aveyron at the Revolution).

Najac itself is an entrancing bastide, set on a virtually impregnable height beside a large meander of the River Aveyron. The counts of Toulouse relied on its fortress to defend the border between the Rouergue and Aquitaine. Parts of this formidable building still stand: a square Romanesque keep guarding its south-west flank, maybe dating from the eleventh century; a thirteenth-century tower, this one circular; four circular towers which once defended the corners of Najac's walls; and the main town gate, the thirteenth century *porte de la Pique* which in the past was merely one of six. Alphonse de Poitiers incorporated all this into the bastide he created here in the 1250s.

The Gothic church is almost as powerful, especially its hexagonal belfry. Built between 1258 and 1280, it stands as a testimony to the skills of the local masons, whose names we know (Bérenguier Jornet, Estève de Canillac and Jean de Villeneuve). A ridge runs east from the ancient centre of the town towards the Ségala plateau, leading to the the market square, which is arcaded and surrounds a fountain. The half-timbered upper storeys of several of the houses are supported on stone pillars, to create the arcades beneath them.

Alphonse de Poitiers gave Najac its charter of rights and duties in 1253, a year after he had reasserted his authority against its rebelliousness by founding Villefranche-de-Rouergue. This major bastide was thus created above all for political and military reasons. In the Rouergue the new bastide was to be his administrative centre and a symbol of his power.

Alphonse instructed Jean d'Arcis, his seneschal in the Rouergue, to purchase a hilly site on the right bank of the Aveyron on which to build the bastide. The urgency with which he needed to attract loyal vassals to

Villefranche-de-Rouergue is attested by his issuing a mere four years after founding the new town a charter setting out their privileges and their various exemptions from taxes. Villefranche-de-Rouergue was to be administered by consuls and had the right to hold markets and fairs.

In 1260 building began on the massive collegiate church of Notre-Dame, though its tower was not completed till 1581. In 1320 the consuls built an irregular, three-arched bridge across the Aveyron (which was restored in the eighteenth century). From here the narrow rue de la République (once called rue Droite, in recognition of the aim of those who built bastides to avoid wherever possible a bend in the road) runs north to the main square of Villefranche-de-Rouergue, place Notre-Dame. The street is flanked by half-timbered houses with twin dormer windows. Ahead appears the massive tower of the bastide's greatest church. From this angle Villefranche-de-Rouergue is lozenge-shaped, with the streets running off at right angles to rue de la République, while in turn other streets and *ruelles* (known in the local patois as *cantou*) run off from them in chequerboard fashion.

Over the centuries Villefranche-de-Rouergue prospered, and in consequence its streets are shaded by fine houses of successive eras, some boasting Gothic façades, others Renaissance staircases. But a walk around the old quarters still reveals, in street names and buildings, classic features of a medieval bastide. Before rue de la République reaches place Notre-Dame, rue de la Monnaie runs off to the left. Its name is a reminder of the mint which existed here till 1556, for the bastide was given the right to strike its own money. Rue de la Monnaie reaches the church of Sainte-Emilie-de-Rodat (named after the foundress of the order of the Holy Family, who lived from 1787 to 1852 and is buried here). From the start this bastide sheltered many religious people, and though this church was consecrated only in 1958, its crypt is ancient, once part of the thirteenth-century monastery belonging to disciples of Saint Francis of Assisi.

Turn right here and you come to the place de la Fontaine, a vital source of water in a bastide that might one day have to submit to siege. The square is enhanced by a monumental open-air staircase as well as by the fourteenth-century fountain. Walk on along rue du Sergent Bories towards the market square. Balconies, some belonging to half-timbered houses, overhang the street. The finest house in this street was built around 1490 for a rich merchant of the town named Guillaume Vedel and is readily recognizable by the wavy porch of its doorway, its sculpted windows and its staircase tower.

Just beyond it, the cobbled place Notre-Dame is arcaded on all four sides, the houses dating from the thirteenth to the nineteenth centuries. The finest house on the north side has double gables. On the south side the finest is a Renaissance mansion with a staircase giving on to an interior courtyard. And on a corner of the east side stands the collegiate church of Notre-Dame, its 58-metre-high fortified belfry rising from a massive overhanging porch. On Thursdays it looks down on the bastide's traditional market.

Inside, the church is a splendid example of Languedoc Gothic, enriched by 62 late fifteenth-century choir stalls sculpted by André Sulpice. The earliest part of the collegiate church is the choir, whose slender windows have fifteenth-century stained glass.

André Sulpice also carved exquisite stalls for the bastide's Charterhouse of the Holy Saviour, which stands outside the main town. Paid for by the widow of Vézian Valette, a local merchant who died on a pilgrimage to Rome, and built between 1450 and 1465, the work led by two master masons from Cordes (Conrad Rogier and Jean Coupiac), its chapel enshrines fifteenth century stained glass in which you can spy the donors adoring the Madonna and Child. Its exquisite little cloister, chapter house and refectory are built in the flamboyant Gothic style, while the great cloister is scarcely less exhilarating.

From the north-west corner of place Notre-Dame runs rue Saint-Jacques, which leads to the chapel and former hospice of Saint James, built to shelter pilgrims who made Villefranche-de-Rouergue a major staging post on the way to Santiago de Compostela. Today the inscription on its lintel reads 'Hôtel de la Charité'. Beyond it is another example of the wealth of this bastide put to pious use. Built in the second half of the seventeenth century in the form of a Greek cross, the chapel of the convent of the Black Penitents contains a gilded, Spanish baroque high altar. Another seventeenth-century foundation at Villefranche-de-Rouergue is the chapel of the Blue Penitents.

In spite of this wealth of devotion, Bishop Raymond de Calmont of Rodez was incensed at the foundation of the bastide. It threatened his revenues, by luring men and women away from farms which he taxed. In addition, the profitable merchants' routes would no longer be bringing wealth to his own coffers. Thirdly, the power of the laity was here encroaching on the dominance of the church. Accordingly the bishop excommunicated the first settlers in the new bastide and in 1280 went so far as to found a rival one of his own.

La Bastide-l'Evêque lies due east of Villefranche-de-Rouergue, and it too is set on an escarpment of the Ségala. Perfectly regular in plan, it is scarcely more than a village. Its finest feature is the parish church, built out of roughly-hewn stones, itself dominated by a powerful belfry at one corner of which rises the staircase tower. In no way could or did La Bastide-l'Evêque rival Villefranche-de-Rouergue; but its existence demonstrates the fierce rivalry for power which prevailed throughout the era of the bastides. Shortly that rivalry would become bloodthirsty.

Royal
Bastides

King Louis VIII of France reigned for a mere three years from 1223. In that short time this forceful sovereign wrested back from the English lands in the Saintonge and the Poitou. In the last year of his life Louis VIII also conquered Aquitaine and the Languedoc, making Raymond VII of Toulouse his vassal.

Two of his sons inherited his vigour. His eldest son, later to be canonized as Saint Louis, inherited the throne of France in 1226. If Louis IX was an innovative creator of bastides, his younger brother was yet greater. Alphonse, third son of Louis VIII and six years younger than Louis IX, was born in 1220. His father made him count of Poitiers.

When Louis IX became king, he forced Raymond VII of Toulouse to accept the Treaty of Meaux, which brought the Cathar lands back under the suzerainty of the French monarchy. To set a dynastic seal on the treaty, his brother Alphonse later married Jeanne de Toulouse, the daughter and sole heir of Count Raymond VII. When Raymond died in 1249, Alphonse de Poitiers became Count Alphonse II of Toulouse.

Alphonse was thus not only a leading member of a family determined to set its realms in order after the confusion and sometimes near-anarchy of the past century; he was also the heir of two bastide-building dynasties. As a convinced Catholic he also shared Louis IX's passion for crusades. In 1248, Alphonse accompanied Louis on ill-starred the Seventh Crusade and, like his brother, was captured, and imprisoned at Mansourah in 1250.

On his return he found his own domains in disarray. To bring order and to restore his own authority to them, Alphonse turned to the device invented by his father-in-law Count Raymond VII of Toulouse. Indefatigably he set about founding bastides for deliberately political reasons. By the end of his life some fifty guarded his domains.

The gift of peace and order was welcome to many throughout those hitherto turbulent lands. Monasteries and local seigneurs were ready to devolve some of their rights by an act of *paréage*, or sharing. Not only were lands shared; so sometimes was the right to collect duties and revenues. Often, however, the charters which the founders granted to anyone who would people their fortified new towns exempted these citizens from taxes. In other cases a charter granting the citizens security, liberty, the right to farm parcels of land and to own, build and buy property was more than enough to attract families to a new foundation.

Alphonse de Poitiers's particular contribution to the genre was a shrewd eye for siting bastides either beside major rivers (as we have already noted at Villefranche-de-Rouerge) or where they could strategically dominate important routes. Among the latter was Villefranche-de-Lauragais, which he founded south-east of Toulouse on the way to the Rhône, to Beaucaire and to Louis IX's bastide at Carcassonne.

Many of the still exquisite bastides Alphonse created lie today in the *département* of Lot-et-Garonne. One such is Villeréal, a town of half-timbered houses, some of them built out of slender red bricks, close by the River Dropt where prehistoric men and women had once made their home and the Romans had built a fort. It lay in a line of French bastides which defended the limits of French territories in the face of those claimed by the English in Périgord. In former times its walls were defended by eight towers as well as a deep ditch, but these ramparts have long disappeared.

Alphonse de Poitiers founded his bastide here in 1267, having con-cluded a *paréage* two years previously with the abbot of Aurillac and Count Gaston de Gontaud-Biron which brought him a forested hill-site. Clause I of its charter, granted to the bastide on 1 May, 1289, declared that no taxes should be levied on its citizens, by either the founder or his successors, nor should they be forced to loan him anything, save of their own free will. Clause II gave the citizens the right freely to dispose of their own goods and furniture. Clause III gave them the right to marry off their daughters or to let them become nuns. Clause XXIII decreed that men and women caught committing adultery should parade naked through the streets. The bailiffs and consuls were given power to punish anyone who threw rubbish in the streets. Clause XXXV granted Villeréal the right to hold a Saturday market.

Today, Villeréal also hosts a Wednesday market in its central square, which is flanked by overhanging, arcaded houses (as well as an early twentieth century town hall), selling clothing, vegetables, fruit and honey. The roof of the market hall is borne on massive oak beams, some of them 15 metres long, rising from a stone base. Inside the hall, its sides open as are nearly all those in classic bastides, a staircase rises to the administrative centre of Villeréal, a half-timbered upper storey where the elected representatives of its citizens would deliberate and take counsel. Its present form dates from the fourteenth and seventeenth centuries.

From this central square run eight principal streets, set at right angles to each other. The fourteenth century church stands an angle to the former corn market and a little way off. Its later Gothic porch bears statues, much mutilated by the Protestants who occupied Villeréal in 1569 and 1572. Dedicated to Notre Dame, the church is fortified, its right hand tower pierced with slits through which archers could shoot at invaders, and connected by a gallery to the tower on the left. This one was powerful enough to double up as the local prison. In past times the church was further protected by a surrounding ditch. Inside, the church is spanned by an early Gothic ceiling.

The name Villeréal denotes that the foundation of this bastide was by a count of royal blood. Twelve kilometres away, as part of the defences of the River Dropt, which here marked the boundary between the English and the French domains, Alphonse de Poitiers had already founded Castillonnès. This spot, on a ridge overlooking the river, had belonged to the abbey of Cadouin in the Dordogne, which became rich by attracting pilgrims to venerate a kerchief claimed to have covered the face of Jesus as he lay in the tomb, which had been brought to France after the First Crusade (and in 1934 was discovered to be a late eleventh-century cloth whose inscription invokes the name of Allah). The foundation of Castillonnès made the monks of Cadouin yet richer, since they were granted the right to take tithes from its citizens.

Najac's thirteenth-century château still guards the town and dominates its valley.

Many times restored, this house in Najac is still redolent
of times past.

Ancient stones at Montfort (named after the dreaded
Simon de Montfort) are these days held together not
with earth but with mortar, and embellished with flowers.

Penne's medieval fortress is perched meanacingly above
the Aveyron gorge.

Few would expect to get the better of this typical Périgord lady by bargaining on market day; yet usually such apparently calculating faces break into smiles of welcome if a visitor simply cries 'Bonjour'.

The arcades of bastides shelter the inhabitants from both cold and heat.

Cobbled streets rise from the fortified gateways of Cordes.

Even when protecting their windows, the citizens of the medieval town of Sarlat do so with style.

Not far from the bastide of Domme, the sculpted walls of medieval Sarlat crumble gently in the afternoon sun.

As here, just outside the place de la Liberté, Sarlat is crammed with medieval houses whose owners have continually embellished them with dormers and staircase towers.

The arcaded central square of Monpazier, the best
preserved bastide in the Dordogne.

An ancient Dordogne statue graces a typical Dordogne window. Note that the window frame has been chiselled by hand, and that the house is built of irregular, uncut stones.

*Sheltered by Monpazier's market hall, the ancient
measures for weighing out grain remain intact.*

*Cap firmly pressed on his head and wearing the
traditional blue trousers of the region's farmers, this
inhabitant of Monpazier returns home with the day's
freshly-baked bread.*

*The delicately fretted roof of the market hall at
Villefranche-du-Périgord.*

Rue Porte de la Combe, running from the ancient fountain of the bastide of Domme to one of its three fortified gates, is a rare peaceful spot in the tourist season.

These romantic turrets of the upper city of Carcassonne look down on the bastide, which is the lower city.

Fleurs-de-lis and carved heads entrance the visitor to Carcassone.

A half-timbered brick house, over an arcade, at
Villeréal, the bastide which Alphonse de Poitiers
founded on the left bank of the River Dropt in 1269.

After centuries of neglect, the splendid bastide of Cordes
is today cherished by its inhabitants.

*The fortified thirteenth-century church of Villeréal rises
above pantiled roofs.*

Beneath ancient bastide walls, the inhabitants play boules.

A corner of Hastingues, a bastide founded by Edward I of England in 1289 and fortified by John de Hastings, who gave it his name.

The abbey's tithe house still exists at Castillonnès, embedded in the buildings around its irregular corn market, the place des Cornières. The new governors of Castillonnès soon took over the building. The arcades of the square are also irregular, some round, some pointed, some almost square, others with flat tops rising on pillars. As at Villeréal the church is slightly offset from the central square.

In terms of military tactics, Castillonnès was built to dominate the route from Bergerac to Agen. Further south, Alphonse strengthened his defences of his lands by building bastides along the valley of the Lède. Here the hillside site of Monflanquin rises to 180 metres. Alphonse acquired the site in 1252, by an act of *paréage* with Guillaume Amanieu, lord of Calviac (an act which is today preserved in the Public Record Ofice, London). His bastide is dominated by its fortified, early Gothic church. The interior boasts a seventeenth-century brick Gothic ceiling, whose arches rise from capitals borne on stone pillars. Behind the high altar is an ambulatory, a curved passage which allowed pilgrims access to small chapels, each of which would have contained a holy relic which the pilgrims would venerate. Beyond the church a natural balcony gives a panorama over the fertile countryside where the fortunate inhabitants of the bastide cultivated their plots of land.

At Monflanquin the church of Saint André, which was built between 1260 and 1290, stands outside the arcaded and tree-shaded corn market, whose site is sloped. Here some of the picturesque houses are half-timbered, the later ones built of stone. From above, the boundaries of Monflanquin resemble a slightly misshapen egg; but within its boundaries the streets and narrower passages (known here as *carrérots*) run from each other in rigidly chequerboard fashion. Some of the *carrérots*, down which in the past escaped dirty water, are a mere 80 centimetres wide. Although the market hall of Monflanquin was demolished in the eighteenth century, its grain measures still survive.

Alphonse de Poitiers's charter of customs, issued in 1256, begins: 'Alphonse to you who read these letters, Greetings. Know that to the inhab-itants of our bastide of Monflanquin in the diocese of Agen we accord the liberties and costumes announced in what follows.' He then gave his new bastide the right to hold a Thursday market. Citizens' liberties were guaran-teed. They were to be governed by six Catholic consuls, drawn from their own ranks in addition to those chosen by the founder's bailiff. These consuls could levy a tax to repair roads, bridges, streets and fountains. They served for one year, unpaid. In 1269, Alphonse issued another charter confirming these privileges and customs, and also giving the community lands outside the walls of the bastide.

In return the count expected the loyalty of the inhabitants of his bastide, above all their willingness to serve him in time of war. Thus a bastide offered mutual benefits, to founder and citizens. It was designed to cement them in a strong bond – in theory, though not always in practice, for on the one hand the bailiffs of the bastides usually exercised more power than the consuls, and the citizens often felt free to change sides under any military threat.

The year of Monflanquin's first charter, 1256, in fact witnessed an extraordinary burst of creative energy by Alphonse de Poitiers. In that year he founded the bastide of Montclar by the river of the same name (cutting corners by giving Montclar the same charter as that of Monflanquin), as well as Lavardac, further south-west.

In that same year he founded Monclar-d'Agenais, also in the *département* of Lot-et-Garonne. Once more his penchant for defensive sites made him seize on one occupied in prehistoric times and by the Romans. Its 187-metre eminence commands the valleys of the rivers Lot and Tolzat. Because of its strategic importance, in the Middle Ages this spot, relatively insignificant today, became one of the most important towns in the region of Agen. Opposite the town hall in its market square is a row of arcades, and its sixteenth century church has an impressive porch. Alphonse's charter attracted citizens to Monclar-d'Agenais by giving them the right to work the local quarries and exploit the surrounding forests.

Lavardac, another foundation of the same year, once more inhabits the site of a Gallo-Roman fort. This bastide commanded the route from the Garonne to the Pyrenees. Blessed with chequerboard streets, its overgrown ramparts tumble down to the River Baïse.

In the meantime 1256 also saw Alphonse founding the delightful bastide of Eymet, around a twelfth-century Benedictine priory at the south-west tip of the Dordogne. A strategically sited new town, like the others founded by this count, Eymet lies in the valley of the Dropt. The bastide suffered many depredations in subsequent centuries, but its citizens repeatedly rebuilt their homes, sometimes in wattle and daub, sometimes in stone. Specializing in fruit, preserves and vegetables, its Thursday market is still held in the splendid place des Arcades, whose fountain was embellished in the present monumental fashion in 1830. Around the square sturdy wooden pillars support half-timbered houses, while the stone houses are carried on pointed arches. Nearby its much restored Romanesque church rise the remains of a fourteenth-century fortress, and the fortifications include a round thirteenth-century watchtower.

Westward, just outside the present *département* of the Dordogne and in the Gironde, Alphonse set up another bastide beside a Benedictine priory founded in the ninth century. Like Eymet, it lies beside a river – this one the Dordogne itself. Some of the fortifications and the arcaded central square, surrounded by covered walkways under the houses, still remain at Sainte-Foy-la-Grande. As its name makes clear, the bastide is built on land which belonged to the monastery of Sainte-Foy at Conques. As we have already seen, over the centuries invaders destroyed many of the ancient houses of the bastide, which the citizens valiantly rebuilt. The best of the older ones are to be seen in rue de la République and rue des Frères Reclus, some of them embellished with carvings.

As for the southern approaches of his capital, Alphonse defended them by founding in 1257 the bastide of Saint-Sulpice-sur-Lèze, once more strategically sited on a river. This bulwark of Toulouse was augmented in 1270, when Alphonse's seneschal founded the bastide of Gaillac-Toulza a few kilometres south-east. Gaillac-Toulza, though a treat, has not preserved many traces of the typical bastide, but at Saint-Sulpice-sur-Lèze you can still trace the regular plan of the original foundation, while the corn market (now the place de la Mairie) still preserves its customary arcades, sheltering walks under half-timbered houses.

Some of the bastides created by the initiative of Alphonse de Poitiers constituted major contributions to the urban transformation of south-west France. His greatest legacy of superb new towns is to be discovered in the adjoining *départements* of Tarn-et-Garonne and Lot-et-Garonne. In the first of these *départements* the indefatigable count founded no fewer than nine, not all of which retain their classic bastide form. Founded in 1271 with the count's brilliant strategic eye, Varennes still overlooks from its hilltop site parts of the valleys of both the Tarn and the Tescou, but the pattern of streets and the fortifications it once possessed are no more.

Another of his foundations, Angeville, is beautifuly sited beside the River Sère and retains many elements to delight a visitor, in particular its sixteenth-century church; but those features special to a thirteenth-century bastide have disappeared. At Monclar-de-Quercy, which was granted its charter by Alphonse de Poitiers in 1267, the church was rebuilt in the late 1870s in the neo-Gothic style. Beside the River Séoune, Montjoi, a village which the count fortified the following year, merely retains vestiges of its wall, a fourteenth-century gate, some sixteenth-century houses and a seventeenth-century château. Molières, which Alphonse founded in 1270 and to whose citizens he granted a charter, has a lovely square and some fine houses, as well as a Renaissance porch on the seventeenth-century church of Saint Nazaire-le-Vieux; but it no longer resembles a medieval bastide. Nor does nearby Mirabel.

On the other hand, fortified Verfeil which lies on the banks of the Seye and overlooks also the valley of the Baye, though much assailed in later centuries, has preserved a medieval gate in what remains of its ramparts, as well as the arcaded square first built in the thirteenth century. Similarly Dunes, which Alphonse founded around 1270, has a church dedicated to Saint Mary Magdalen, parts of which date back to the fourteenth century, though its present Toulouse-type belfry was built only in 1848. Here is an arcaded market square and vestiges of its fortifications. And Castelsagrat, which Alphonse founded two years later to guard stretches of both the River Séoune and the River Barguelonne, retains a Romanesque well, a picturesque arcaded central square, and the medieval Gothic church of the Blessed

Virgin Mary. Surrounding the church are some of those typical arcaded bastide houses.

As for the *département* of Lot-et-Garonne, apart from those bastides we have already encountered, Count Alphonse founded Labastide-Castel-Amouroux in 1269 on a hillock commanding the route from Casteljaloux to Marmande. Today its thirteenth-century church is its chief attraction, especially the heads and foliage which adorn its tympanum, the capitals which decorate the colonettes of the porch, and the monsters and human heads carved on the doorway of the staircase tower.

In the same year came Laparade, which Alphonse named Castelseigneur and where you can still sit in the central square and also find traces of the former fortifications. Obtaining the land from the Benedictines of Clairac (the remains of their abbey can still be seen a few kilometres to the south-west), Alphonse sited his bastide here to dominate the valleys of the Lot and the Torgue, and in consequence the town today offers magnificent panoramas of these rivers and the surrounding countryside. Walls still surround the little town. Two wells flank its nineteenth-century church; and if you walk along rue 8 Mai 1945 to place Gabaret you will discover half-timbered houses.

Tournon-d'Agenais on the edge of the Lot followed in 1270. Dominating the valley of the River Boudoyssou, it stands on a hill reached by hairpin bends. The arcaded market square has a well, vital for the citizens' survival in time of siege. At one corner rises a venerable white stone belfry and clock tower. Damazan, north-west of Agen, with its rectangular layout, the towers of its former ramparts, its arcaded central square and corn market, is another of Alphonse's foundations in the same *département*. It was created in his marathon year of 1256 on land bought from the abbey of Fontgailleau. On the north-east side of the square and set at an angle rises the fourteenth-century church, restored five hundred years later.

Saint-Pastour, the smallest bastide in the whole Agen region, lies south-west of Monflanquin. Though it has preserved vestiges of its walls and one of its ancient gates, as well as the ruins of its château, the place is dominated by its church, built in the late twelfth century before the foundation of the bastide. In front of the church is the town's well; inside it are the workings of an old clock, constructed between 1600 and 1630. Alphonse de Poitiers founded this bastide in 1272. Two main streets, running east–west, bisect the bastide, and between them is the old, wooden market hall, oddly enough not in the middle of a square. Saint-Pastour received its charter of customs from King Edward 1 of England in 1289. The most innovative feature was the declaration that serious differences between citizens ought not to be settled by duels.

If Eymet in the Dordogne is probably the prettiest bastide founded by Alphonse de Poitiers, Villeneuve-sur-Lot in the Lot-et-Garonne is the biggest. It is reached from Saint-Pastour by way of Sainte-Livrade-sur-Lot, which began life as a Benedictine priory founded in 1116 by the monastery of La Chaisse-Dieu. The priory church, its oldest parts dating back to the twelfth century, is built of long, narrow bricks. Today the oldest part is the apse, while the transepts, the nave and the belfry date from the fourteenth century, some parts rebuilt in the nineteenth. Inside are seventeenth-century canons' stalls. Unlike the rest of the church, the apse is built of stone. The outside of the apse has blind arcades with fine capitals, from which rises a second storey as far as a magnificent cornice decorated with Romanesque carvings of animals and humans, some of them decaying. Beyond it rises a simple market hall, and the stalls of the bi-monthly fairs stretch between it and the apse of the parish church.

Set among hillsides covered with vines and orchards, Villeneuve-sur-Lot again derives from a Benedictine abbey. But its antecedents are much older, dating back as far as a Gallo-Roman colony which commanded a Roman crossroads, where the route from Périgueux to Agen met that from Cahors to Bordeaux. Archaeologists have uncovered Roman remains here, including a former temple. With the intention of building a major new town here, Alphonse de Poitiers purchased nearly thirty hectares of land from the abbot of Eysses and the baron of Pujols. The abbey of Eysses, a mere two kilometres from Villeneuve-sur-Lot on the way to Monflanquin, was rebuilt in the seventeenth century and now serves as a prison, visitable only by convicted criminals, their gaolers and their families. As for Pujols, which rises on a hill three kilometres south of the new bastide, it had suffered so grievously during the Albigensian crusade that its château had been demolished and many of its inhabitants expelled, dispossessed of their homes and livelihoods.

Attracted by Alphonse's charter of rights at Villeneuve-sur-Lot, issued in 1270, they found protection inside the bastide's powerful fortifications of which remain the *portes de Paris* and *de Pujols*, both of them built in the thirteenth century and strengthened in the fifteenth. The 30 metre-high tower of the former rises from a stone base, the next three storeys brick. Apart from the archway enabling citizens to pass in and out, the only openings in its walls are the encorbellments which enabled those inside to rain missiles down on any invader. The equally powerful *porte de Pujols* guards the southern entrance to the bastide 700 metres away.

Between 1282 and 1289 a bridge was thrown across the Lot (today matched by two modern ones and now called rue des Cientat). In the past this ancient bridge was guarded by three crenellated towers, all of them now gone. In 1642 a flood demolished the arch nearest the right bank, which was rebuilt. Buttressed in the eighteenth century, this bridge had enormous economic importance for Villeneuve-sur-Lot, for centuries bringing travellers and merchants to the bastide, since it improved the route from Auch to Périgueux.

It also enabled the bastide to develop on both sides of the river. The suburb on the left bank is smaller, semi-circular, but with the parcels of land offered to new inhabitants much the same as those in the rectangular main city on the right bank. Both parts of the bastide are set out chequerboard fashion. Beside the ancient bridge stands the chapel of Notre-Dame-de-Gauch (Our Lady of Joy), rebuilt at the beginning of the sixteenth century when the nearby tower guarding the bridge collapsed and the whole building fell into the river. Its reredos, pulpit and paintings all date from the seventeenth-century restoration.

At Villeneuve-sur-Lot the corn market was held in what is today called place La Fayette. Still surrounded by arcaded passageways, it boasts an elaborate Renaissance fountain. Part of the charm of this corn market derives from the variety of its arcades, the north and west sides each with seven arches, those on the north particularly irregular. On the south side there are five, one of them ogival. Most of the houses flanking this square date from the seven-teenth and eighteenth centuries, rebuilt after the troubles of the Fronde.

Beyond the square stands the octagonal, Toulouse-style tower of the spacious parish church. But this church, dedicated to Saint Catherine of Alexandria and built of red brick, is an oddity at Villeneuve-sur-Lot. Towards the end of the nineteenth century the fabric of the bastide's first church was in a dangerous condition. Instead of restoring it the citizens decided to build a new one, choosing an architect named Corroyer who was renowned for his work at Mont-Saint-Michel. He decided to build in the Romanesque-Byzantine style, using brick, granite and white stones to give variety to his new church. Work began in 1898, and when it finished in 1909 the old church was demolished.

In the windows of the new building was inserted the fifteenth- and sixteenth-century stained glass of the old one. This is an ensemble of Gothic and Renaissance glass, fascinating in its iconography. As one would expect, they depict scenes from the life of the patroness of the church, Saint Cather-ine, together with the martyrdom of Saint Foy. As Villeneuve-sur-Lot was initially a Benedictine foundation, Saint Benedict appears, too. Apart from scenes which could scarcely be omitted from any stained glass of this epoch (the Madonna and Child, her mother Saint Anne, Saint Laurence being grilled to death), they also portray the patron saints of the various craftsmen of the town: Eloi, patron of silverworkers, with a silversmith's hammer; Peter, called from his fishing nets by Jesus and thus the patron saint of fishermen and sailors. Finally, Saint James the Great appears three times, for Villeneuve-sur-Lot inevitably attracted pilgims on their way to his Spanish shrine. One of these portraits even depicts a pilgrim, kneeling before the Saint.

In the pedestrianized streets of modern Villeneuve-sur-Lot you notice medieval houses, for example at no. 12 rue Parmentier (which is named after the culinary pioneer who brought the potato to France). Sometimes three storeys high, the second storey can be built of narrow red brick with timbering, the upper storey plastered. Such a house, on the corner of rue Arnaud Daubisse, has been recently embellished with a statue of Saint Catherine of Alexandria, standing on the wheel on which her tormentors tried to break her.

At no. 14 rue de la Convention a plaque identifies the former Viguerie or court house of Villeneuve-sur-Lot. This unpretentious half-timbered building, whose upper storey overhangs the street, was built in 1264. In the same street are more lovely half-timbered houses, some of them (as is the former Viguerie) nowadays restaurants.

Villeneuve, or new town, is obviously as suitable a term for a bastide as Villefranche. In the Aveyron, north of Villefranche-de-Rouergue, is a bastide called simply Villeneuve. This is one of those bastides which developed out of a *sauveté*, in the case of Villeneuve from one founded in 1053 by the Benedictine Pierre I Bérenger, abbot of Rodez. Its charter required the inhabitants to build him a priory here, which was finished by the end of the century. Dedicating the priory church to the Holy Saviour, they built it in a circular fashion, to remind them of the church of the Holy Sepulchre in Jerusalem.

Situated beside the River Algouse, Villeneuve boasts two town gates, the first a powerful square one, and the second machicolated. The former leads straight into the irregular, tree-shaded place des Conques. Arcaded, surrounding a well, the square preserves its ancient grain measures; some of the houses date from the fifteenth and sixteenth centuries; and the once entirely circular Romanesque church was enlarged in the fourteenth with a nave and embellished with frescoes. Its octagonal belfry, built in the Romanesque era, was also added to in the fourteenth century.

The thirteenth-century frescoes decorating the apse of Saint-Sauveur at Villeneuve almost compete in fascination with the stained glass windows at Villeneuve-de-Rouergue. Jesus is painted here, surrounded by the symbols of the four evangelists. In medallions are portraits of the twelve apostles. To the jaded palate of the twentieth-century traveller who has seen so much, these exquisite works of medieval art can seem merely run-of-the-mill, though they are certainly not so. What brings one short with amazement is a section depicting pilgrims (presumably to Santiago de Compostela), remarkably depicted in their different social classes just as Chaucer did verbally in his *Canterbury Tales*.

West of Pamiers, in the *département* of the Ariège, a dependency of the lords of Durfort took the name Villeneuve-du-Latou after being transformed into a bastide in the thirteenth century. Washed by the River Midou east of Mont-de-Marsan, is Villeneuve-de-Marsan, its fortified fourteenth century church still sheltering a bastide which in the thirteenth century took the place of a town founded in the tenth century. Vestigial sixteenth century frescoes inside the church depict the life of Saint Catherine of Alexandria. The capitals are worth pausing over. In the winter months the market is even more agreeable, selling the luscious *foie gras* produced by the local farmers. And throughout its history the bastide has been defended by a thirteenth-century tower which was crenellated a hundred years later.

Among the bastides which encircle the city of Albi is Villeneuve-sur-Vère. Its present name derives from the river beside which it was built, but in past times the bastide was known as Villeneuve-la-Nouvelle, to distinguish it from an older town on the other side of the river destroyed by the Albigensian crusaders.

The title Villeneuve also takes us to a far more easterly part of France than we have hitherto visited. Villeneuve-de-Berg is in the Cévennes, in the *département* of the Drôme, scarcely ten kilometres from the River Rhône. Lavender, vines and orchards flourish on the slopes of its rocky plateau. In 1284, King Philippe III le Hardi made an agreement with the monks of the powerful Cistercian monastery at Mazan to build a bastide here. Speedily issuing a charter of duties, rights and privileges, he managed to entice families to populate his new town within six years.

Once again the Capetian monarchy had chosen to build a defensive town on a site at a strategic point on a major route, this one between Viviers and Aubenas. The old town is set out in the customary geometrical fashion of a bastide. Architecturally, the parish church proclaims the austerity of

Cistercian monasticism, which eschewed arrogance and ostentatious embellishment. Today its rich furnishings – a baroque pulpit and baroque reredoses – seem curiously at odds with this ideal.

As ever, the industrious citizens of the bastide brought prosperity to the surrounding countryside. Villeneuve-de-Berg is especially proud of Olivier de Serres, who was born here in 1539 and promoted the cultivation of mulberry trees and silkworms. In the place de la Halle the citizens in 1804 erected a pyramid in his honour, for some reason resting on four ox heads. In the fourth centenary of his birth, they set up a statue of Olivier on the belvedere of the bastide which looks out over the hazy hills of the Cévennes.

Mention of Philippe le Hardi brings us back to the powerful founders of these new towns. Alphonse de Poitiers died in 1271 on his return from the Eighth Crusade. Before quitting his memory, we should acknowledge the Alaman family, who served among his most important lieutenants and were active alongside him in founding bastides. Villeneuve-sur-Vère in the *département* of the Tarn was founded in the mid-thirteenth century by Déodat d'Alaman.

Another member of this family, Sicard I d'Alaman, had also served Raymond VII of Toulouse, founding on his behalf the bastide of Castelnau-de-Lévis in the Tarn in 1235. Raymond needed a bastion on this spot, a hill-site known as the Puy de Bonnafous, in order to protect himself against Albi, ceded to the king of France in 1229. Unusually, therefore, as well as a bastide Sicard was allowed to construct a powerful fortress here, which was finished in 1256 – the year his bastide gained its charter of customs.

Castelnau-de-Lévis was initially called Castelnau-de-Bonnafous, after the hill on which it stands. By one of those dynastic arrangements whereby formerly warring factions in France reconciled their differences, in 1297 one of Sicard's descendants married Philippe de Lévis, himself a descendant of Simon de Montfort. Thus the bastide passed definitively into the royal domain, and its citizens replaced the name Bonnafous with that of the Lévis family.

On land north of Toulouse, which had belonged to the Hospitallers of Saint-Jean-de-Garidech, Sicard d'Alaman was also responsible for founding in 1242 Montastruc-la-Conseillière, a bastide which became a dependency of the French crown thirty years later. Thus, slowly but consistently, the kings of France obliterated the historical and dynastic legacy of the Cathars.

Philippe III le Hardi (the bold) succeeded to the throne of France in 1270, on the death of his father Louis IX in the Holy Land. A year after his accession to the throne he received the vast patrimony of his uncle, Alphonse de Poitiers.

Inevitably Philippe sought to consolidate his hold by founding bastides, the finest which is undoubtedly Domme in the Dordogne. After Simon de Montfort had razed the château of the earlier town, Domme-Vielle remained the property of the monks of Sarlat. A little to the east is a rocky spur which rises suddenly and steeply from the flat surrounding countryside and on one side precipitately plunges down to the River Dordogne itself.

Philippe le Hardi acquired the site in 1280, from Guillaume de Domme, a vassal of the monks of Sarlat, paying him 200 livres. He had been dead twenty-five years by the time the bastide was finished in 1310. Partly the delay arose from the difficulties of building on such a site. A second reason was that the countryside, today fertile, was at that time desperately poor. Thirdly, the workers complained that they were obliged to take their pay in leather coinage minted by the king's officers. (The oldest house in the bastide, in the place de la Rode, is inscribed: 'Maison du Batteur de Monnaie du Roy Philippe III le Hardi + 1282 +'.)

On such an irregular, defensive mound, Domme's fortifications inevitably follow the contours of the hill rather than the customary rectangular pattern of a bastide. The ramparts climb around the spur and are pierced by three lovely medieval gates, the smallest the *porte de la Combe*, outside which was once a fountain. The two major defensive gates of Domme are the *porte del Bos*, with its pointed arch still grooved for the portcullis and topped by square-cut stones that seem perilously perched on each other, and the *porte des*

Tours, flanked with massive circular towers which are the main entrances and exits to the town. This gate too was once defended by a portcullis.

Throughout the bastide, ochre houses line narrow and wider streets crossing each other at right angles. Place de la Rode, however, which you climb to either from the *porte de la Combe* or from the *porte del Bos*, is triangular, despite its name which is Occitan for place de la Roue, or wheel. The *roue* in question is the wheel on which malefactors, particularly thieves, brigands and murderers, were once broken here. Follow rue porte des Tours from place de la Rode to find the greatest of the gates of Domme, passing the bastide's second fountain (where a placard declares that the waters are no longer drinkable).

Alternatively, climb from the place de la Rode up the Grand'Rue, to discover on either side of this straight, pedestrianized shopping street handsome houses whose façades display ogival windows. Look right along rue des Consuls (its name deriving from the former elected rulers of Domme) to see the bastide's former town hall, crenellated and with Gothic windows, which dates from the thirteenth century.

The chequerboard streets of Domme can be steep. The most celebrated nineteenth century novelist of the Dordogne was Eugène Le Roy, who earned his living as a tax-collector here. One of his novels, set in Domme, declares that that the womenfolk of this bastide had such shapely legs because of the exercise they found merely traversing its streets. He also eulogizes the egalitarianism brought about by the rights afforded to the citizens. 'In this small spot the distinctions of class were scarcely visible,' he mused. 'Thanks both to its isolation and the difficulty of access which repelled strangers, something of the original equality of the inhabitants had survived, the result of the early charters and by the way the land was parcelled out, and strengthened by the interlocking relationships of families that had frequently intermarried.' In pride and in gratitude for his praise of the town, Domme has affixed a commemorative plaque on the house in which he lived (which stands in the middle of rue Eugène Le Roy).

Grand'Rue climbs to the heart of the bastide, the place de la Halle. On the right rises the governor's house, encorbelled and with its impressive square tower, decorated with turrets. Built in the fifteenth century, this *hôtel du Gouverneur* now wears a seventeenth-century façade. At the centre of the square rises the market hall, built in the seventeenth century, with powerful, honey-coloured stone pillars rising to an elegant wooden balcony. The hall is roofed not with tiles but with *lauzes*, sliced stones steeply set one above the other. Oddly enough, instead of sheltering under this eighteenth-century hall, Domme's Thursday fruit, vegetable and flower market spreads itself out into the square itself. The hall protects not the farmers but a prehistoric cave (to which you can descend). Some 450 metres long, it was once the haunt of palaeolithic people, and in later perilous times protected the citizens who would hide there from invaders.

Just beyond the square, as is so often the case in a bastide, rises the church. Massively fortified, it boasts a high gabled belfry carrying three bells. Restored in the seventeenth century, the church was given a pretty, if incongruous, Renaissance porch. And beyond it is the remarkable drop of some 150 metres directly down to the river. Looking over it at the countryside through which the river meanders, you can see the result of a long transformation of the once inhospitable land around this bastide, with avenues of poplars, clusters of walnut trees, and tilled fields growing wheat, silver clover, maize, tobacco and sainfoin.

Aquitaine and the Midi-Pyrénées owe a good handful of other fine bastides to Philippe le Hardi, though not all of them have survived in such excellent condition as Domme. Still close by the River Dordogne (though a good way north-east of Domme in the *département* of the Lot), he and the Cistercian abbey of Dalon created Puybrun – to the annoyance of the viscount of Turenne, who felt his rights were being infringed and saw his revenues disappearing. Puybrun is still a town with a chequerboard pattern and a thirteenth- and fourteenth-century church.

Further south the king took possession of Nègrepelisse in the Tarn-et-Garonne, attracting by a charter of 1285 the new citizens who built its arcaded square. Nègrepelisse was set in an immense forest, and even derives its name from the sooty skins of the charcoal burners who lived there. Those who built the bastides of Philippe le Hardi seem to have specialized in sites with fine vistas, and the one from Nègrepelisse overlooks the Aveyron gorge and still forested land.

In the previous year, in *paréage* with a local lord and with the aid of his own Toulouse seneschal Eustache de Beaumarchais, Philippe had founded Miélan at what is now the southern tip of the *département* of the Gers. Today its town hall stands where once a market hall sheltered the citizens.

South-east of Miélan, in the Haute-Garonne, he founded Boulogne-sur-Gesse in *paréage* with the nearby abbey of Nizors, giving the bastide its charter in 1286. Just as Miélan derives its name from Milan in Italy, so the new town took its name from Bologna, where the abbot had been educated. Fortified, it was designed to dominate the rivers Gesse and Gimone, rising on a hill site between them. Although the plague severely troubled Boulogne-sur-Gesse and although its fortifications are no more, the central square is still arcaded and surrounded by medieval houses, with the town hall now occupying its market hall. To one side rises the fifteenth-century church, with a Gothic gabled porch.

Still further south, in the same *département*, in *paréage* with the lord of Espagne-Montespan, Philippe le Hardi founded the bastide of Montréjeau. At its foundation in 1272 he decreed its name to be Mont-Royal, or royal mount, for the new town stands on a hill north of the confluence of the rivers Garonne and Neste. Once again, this bastide retains its arcaded central square, as well as medieval houses and the fourteenth-century Gothic church of Saint John, to which an octagonal belfry was added in the seventeenth century. The panoramas from its public garden are almost as fine as those from Domme and Nègrepelisse.

Eustache de Beaumarchais, seneschal of Toulouse from 1270 to 1294, served both Philippe le Hardi and his son Philippe le Bel. A mighty founder of bastides, even before the abbot of Nizors and Philippe le Hardi had developed the penchant for calling their new towns after celebrated foreign cities, Eustache had established the habit. Splendid Fleurance in the Gers is a case in point, taking its name from Florence in Tuscany. In 1272 the local lord of Saint-Puy was desperate for help, for his lands were being ravaged by the count of Armagnac. In *paréage* with him, Eustache founded the bastide, granting the citizens a charter six years later. The site was ideally defensible, a hill known as Montaiglon, bordered on three sides by the River Gers and two streams.

At the heart of the bastide the massive church of Saint Lawrence and the arcaded market square superbly match each other. The church dates from the fourteenth century, the cockleshells on its façade a symbol of Saint James the Great and the pilgrimage to Santiago de Compostela. Its southern side is flanked by a polygonal belfry of the style made popular by the great churches of Toulouse and added to this one in the fifteenth century. Through its fourteenth-century porch you discover that you must descend eight steps into the nave, for over the centuries the soil level outside the church has built up against the walls.

The interior is vast, 70 metres long and 37 metres wide. Undoubtedly the oldest part of the church is its apse, begun in the late thirteenth century. Three entrancing stained glass windows survive of those which were glazed for its apse by Arnaud de Moles in the sixteenth century. The main one depicts the tree of Jesse, that is, Jesus's family tree, with the Madonna and Child at the top and perched in the branches below them King David playing his harp. On the left another window depicts the risen Jesus disguised as a gardener (or at least carrying a spade) while Saint Mary Magdalen kneels before him, having failed to recognize her Lord. In the fragmentary third stained glass window are Saint Augustine and Saint Lawrence, patron of this church, lying on a griddle at his martyrdom, red flames already licking his naked body.

In the nearby place de la République rises the huge arcaded stone market hall with a superb fretwork of beams supporting its roof. This hall was rebuilt in 1834, and simpering nineteenth-century bronze ladies adorn fountains at each corner. The round arches of the powerful stone houses surrounding the hall (some of them with superb wrought-iron balconies) give entrance to covered walks.

Around 1290, Eustache founded another bastide, this one in the Tarn, which he called Pampelonne, after Pamplona in Spain, which he had just captured. He had already founded Saint-Félix-Lauragais in the Haute-Garonne, Valence-d'Albigeois in the Tarn, and Beaumont-de-Lomagne in the Tarn-et-Garonne. The last has a particularly fine chequerboard layout. In place Gambetta, which is arcaded on two sides, stands the fourteenth-century market hall whose pantiled roof rises from wooden pillars. Beaumont-de-Lomagne has some ancient overhanging houses, as well as the splendid brick church of Notre Dame, built between the thirteenth and sixteenth centuries and dominated by its fifteenth-century octagonal belfry.

The marauding Armagnacs against whose depredations Eustache founded Fleurance were themselves not slow in seeing the importance of bastides in consolidating their domains, which included almost all of the present *département* of the Gers. Their capital was Lectoure, a superb town whose glory is the massive former cathedral of Saint Gervais and Saint Proteus. Begun in the fourteenth century, it seems to symbolize the combination of brutal power and courtly grace of that era. In spite of its gorgeous interior, with an ambulatory around the high altar to allow pilgrims to venerate shrines in the elaborately decorated circle of chapels at the east end, the house of God none-the-less remains as powerfully built inside as it does out. Lectoure was once fortified, and some of the fifteenth-century walls remain as well as the contemporary *tour du Bourreau*; it retains the fountain of Diana which succoured its citizens from the thirteenth century; you can still see the remains of the Armagnacs' château; and the town lies only 11 kilometres north of Fleurance whose lord an Armagnac once terrorized.

In 1275, Count Géraud V d'Armagnac founded the bastide of Montfort scarcely 10 kilometres south-east of Fleurance, high on a hill above the River Orbe and protected by brick and stone walls. Red tiled houses line its chequerboard streets. The central square, still bordered with galleried houses, is arcaded on two sides and shelters a market hall which rises from stone and wooden beams. Some of the cool, covered walks have stone arches matching those of the arcades. The thirteenth- and fourteenth-century church, which, unusually, stands in the square itself, has a Gothic octagonal tower, rising three storeys above the church, and a polygonal apse.

Further east the count defended his domains by founding the bastide of Valence-sur-Baïse in 1274, in *paréage* with the abbot of Flaran. Ten years later, in *paréage* with the abbey of la Case-Dieu, Count Bernard v d'Armagnac founded the bastide of Mourède in the same region. Finally, to defend the south-western approaches to their territory, in 1322 in *paréage* with the same abbey Count Jean I d'Armagnac founded the bastide of Plaisance.

If you drive nine kilometres south-east of the Armagnacs' Montfort, you reach the bastide of Mauvezin, set on a hilltop commanding the frontier between Aquitaine and the lands of Narbonne. Mauvezin is not laid out in a chequerboard fashion, but compensates for this by its outstanding market square, where almost all the arcaded houses and covered walks date from the thirteenth century. The market hall is superb, the beams of its roof rising from four rows of stone columns set against one side of the wide square.

Another nine kilometres east of Mauvezin stands the first bastide we have yet seen associated with King Philippe le Bel (the fair), who succeeded his father Philippe le Hardi on the throne of France in 1285. From its name one might guess (rightly) that Eustache de Beaumarchais also had a hand in its foundation, for this bastide is named Cologne.

In 1284, Philippe le Bel charged Eustache to conclude a *paréage* with the local lord, Viscount Odon de Terride. On land bought from the parish of Notre Dame de Sabolène was then built a bastide, whose houses, bastions and market hall are picturesquely constructed of brick, stone, wood and cob. The place de la Halle is set amid nine rectangular or square blocks of houses, their streets running at right angles to each other. Around this central square rise deliciously varied houses, some half-timbered (in contrasting designs), others built of narrow red brick, others plastered. Their lower storeys over-hang a covered way, and even here the supports are diverse – sometimes brick arches, somtimes stone arches, sometimes brick pillars, sometimes stone pil-lars. Other houses set themselves at an angle to the corners of the square.

At the heart of the place de la Halle the fourteenth century market hall rises like a pyramid. At each corner is a stone pillar, the rest being constructed of wood. Above the intricate woodwork of the ceiling rises the beautifully preserved communal hall. Beneath, the market hall shelters a stone grain measure, dating from the fifteenth century. The church of Our Lady in her Assumption stands quite apart from this square, set against the eastern ram-part of the bastide. Much restored and altered, it none-the-less preserves vestiges of its original aspect, particularly its fourteenth-century façade.

Not content with Cologne, Philippe le Bel also founded bastides named after Pavia and Granada. Pavie, created in 1281, lies south of Auch at the confluence of the Gers with the rivers Cédon and Sousson. Grenade is also situated on a river, this one the Garonne north-west of Toulouse. Here is another superb church, brick, partly fortified, with a Gothic porch and an octagonal Toulouse-style belfry surmounted by a steeple. The bastide is abso-lutely rectilinear, its crowning glory the market hall, complex wooden upper storeys rising from octagonal brick pillars.

Philippe le Bel reigned until 1315. His long and energetic reign has left us numerous other bastides, include Briatexte in the Tarn, Labastide-Clermont in the Haute-Garonne, Saint-Denis in the Aude and Réalville in the Tarn-et-Garonne. His second son, Philippe V le Long (who succeeded his brother Louis X in 1316), not only founded the bastide of Galan in the Hautes-Pyrénées but one which was to take the name of another great foreign city. Founded in 1316 in *paréage* with the prior of Saint Gilles, Barcelonne-du-Gers lies at the very tip of the *département* of the Gers.

In energy, ambition and avarice, Philippe le Bel far surpassed the rest of his dynasty. By marriage to Queen Joanna of Navarre he gained Champagne, Navarre and Brie. He persecuted Jews and greedily confiscated their property. He invaded Flanders, unsuccessfully. His attempt to impose taxes on the clergy (in order to raise money for his war against the English) led to a bitter quarrel with Pope Boniface VIII. When Philippe felt strong enough to imprison the bishop of Pamiers, in 1302 the pope summoned the senior clergy of France to a council in Rome, after which he issued a bull asserting the supremacy of the spiritual over the temporal power. Philippe solemnly burned the bull, countering the pope's attack by alleging that Boniface was guilty of sexual misdemeanours and ought to be deposed. In October 1303 Boniface died, miserable and worn out by these struggles.

His successor, Benedict XI, whose reign lasted only from 22 October 1303 to 7 July 1304, was too weak to take on Philippe and granted him the right to two years of clerical tithes. The next pope was a Frenchman, Bertrand de Got, a creature of the king and archbishop of Bordeaux since 1299. Philippe insisted that Bertrand be crowned pope not in Rome but at Lyons. Bertrand complied, taking the name Clement V. In March 1309 the king forced Clement to move his court to Avignon, where it was to remain for seventy years. In 1311 the wretched pope was forced to issue a bull praising Philippe's attacks on Boniface VIII.

Just as he had coveted and plundered the wealth of French Jews,

Philippe now set his sights on the rich possessions of the Knights Templars. They had returned from the Holy Land wealthy and set themselves up as bankers. As we have already seen, they owned property throughout France. Philippe's agents circulated rumours about their homosexual practices, blasphemous rituals and heretical notions – all of these allegations almost certainly false.

On 13 October 1307, every Templar in France was arrested. Tortured, they confessed to innumerable crimes and Philippe had their confessions forwarded to the pope, demanding that the order be condemned. In 1312, Clement complied, assigning their property to the Knights Hospitallers, though Philippe had no qualms about holding on to it till his death. Thousands of Templars were burned as heretics.

A melancholy reminder of the plight of Philippe's victims can be seen today in the bastide of Domme. Between 1307 and 1318 the semicircular towers of the *porte des Tours* served as a prison for condemned Templars. They inscribed on the walls their distinctive crosses, crucifixions, the Holy Grail and their own curious symbols. Here, too, they incised representations of the Blessed Virgin Mary and of Saint John, the Templars' patron saint. Not suprisingly, the doomed prisoners also inscribed curses against Clement v and Philippe le Bel.

The Bastides
in
Times of War

In 1323 the baron of Montpezat, whose territories lay at the very heart of the Lot-et-Garonne, led a group of his followers into the nearby bastide of Saint-Sardos, planning a murder. For several decades the lords of Montpezat had taken the side of the English against the French throne, and since its foundation Saint-Sardos had irked them as a symbol of French royal power only two kilometres away from Monpezat, their own capital.

Sardos is an abbreviation of Sacerdos, a saint who was born in Calviac on the borders of Périgord and the Lot and became bishop of Limoges in the year 515. The saint could cure lepers and was reputed to have raised his own father from the dead. On 5 May 520 he himself died at Argentat, and his corpse was brought down the River Dordogne to Calviac, to be transferred eventually to the abbey church of Sarlat (which is still dedicated to him). In the tenth century the abbey of Sarlat established a priory in the Lot, dedicated to their patron saint, and it was on this spot in 1289 that Philippe le Bel, in *paréage* with the monks of Sarlat, decided to found a bastide.

Work proceeded slowly and was still continuing under Philippe's son and successor Charles IV, who succeeded to the throne in 1322. In many bastides it was the custom to erect a stake on which was displayed the arms of its founder, and one had been erected at Saint-Sardos bearing the royal arms. In 1323 the baron and his followers hanged the royal procurator close by this pole, and then proceeded to pillage and set fire to the bastide.

In later centuries the town restored its fortunes. Lying today among orchards and vineyards, its former priory church preserves a twelfth-century Romanesque porch and some Romanesque capitals, and the children of Saint-Sardos are still baptized in a twelfth-century font hollowed out of another capital. But in 1323, Charles IV took swift reprisals. The following year the château of Montpezat was ravaged. Even so, this little town is still worth a visit, if only for its church of Saint-Jean-de-Balesme. Some of the porches are superbly carved. Inside, the Romanesque exterior is transformed into a two-aisled Gothic church. Under its Romanesque font a mad beast writhes on its back, and Romanesque capitals are on show, fallen from their original perches and laid out on the church floor.

The incident of Saint-Sardos was one of the sparks that ignited the Hundred Years War. Of course the antagonism between the English and the French had simmered for much longer, dating back to 1152 when Louis VII of France dissolved his first marriage. From the start the union had been disastrous. His bride, Eleanor of Aquitaine, was only fifteen years old when they married in 1137, but her dowry was the whole of Aquitaine, inherited from her father. Complaining that she had married a monk, not a king, she none-the-less bore him two daughters. The ill-assorted pair spent two and half years together on the Second Crusade, increasingly aware that their marriage was a failure. Conveniently remembering that they were within the prohibited degrees of relationship, they obtained an annullment.

The young and extremely beautiful Eleanor was now a prized, much-sought-after consort, especially since she still had in her gift the duchy of Aquitaine. Ambitious lords immediately sought her hand in marriage, but she had her own plans and urgently sent messages to Henry Plantagenet, who was not only duke of Normandy and count of Anjou but also the future king of England. On Whit Sunday 1152, a mere eight weeks after the ending of her marriage to Louis, she and Henry were married in the cathedral of Poitiers.

Thus Henry Plantagenet became duke of Aquitaine. To his already extensive lands in France were now added Guyenne and Poitou. Louis VII refused to recognize his claim to these new domains, and Henry spent the autumn of 1153 attempting to enforce his authority throughout his extensive realm. A year later he succeeded to the English throne. He and Eleanor were crowned in Westminster Abbey on 19 December 1154.

Exactly one hundred years later, when the first generation of bastides was being built, a *modus vivendi* between the English and the French seemed to have been worked out. Beginning in 1254, the legates of Louis IX of France and Henry III of England devised a formula which was enshrined in the treaty of Paris, signed by both sovereigns on 4 December 1259. By its provisions, Louis recognized the Plantagenet claim to Gascony, Bordeaux, Bayonne and Périgord. In turn Henry III became a liege of the king of France, and renounced all claims to any other territories, save those of the Agenais and the Quercy. Those were to remain French; but if Jeanne de Toulouse, the wife of Alphonse de Poitiers, were to die without an heir, they would revert to the English crown.

This treaty in part explains the energy Alphonse de Poitiers displayed in creating bastides from the mid-1250s onwards. His *annus mirabilis*, 1256, fell two years after negotiations began over the treaty. Scrutiny of a map of what is now the *département* of the Lot-et-Garonne reveals him constructing a defensive line, running eastwards from the bastide of Tournon-d'Agenais by way of the bastides of Monflanquin, Castelnaud-de-Gratecambe,

Villeneuve-sur-Lot, Saint-Pastour, Laparade, Damazan and Labastide-Castel-Amouroux. From this defensive line three more of his bastides, Villereál, Castillonnès and Eymet, pushed further north towards the English stronghold of Périgord.

The English speedily realized that their own territories were at risk. After signing the treaty of Paris, Henry III was greatly taxed by the problems of England, and so it happened that the first English bastide was founded by his wife, Eleanor of Provence. Monségur in the Gironde, like the French bastides of Villereál, Castillonnès and Eymet, took advantage of the River Dropt as an additional defence to its own fortifications. Eleanor founded her new town, on a 'secure hill' (Mons securus) overlooking the river, around 1265, when it received its charter. Vestiges of its ramparts can still be seen. A Gothic bridge crosses the Dropt here, and the pattern of the streets still follows the regular scheme of the original foundation, as does the rectangular market square.

Eleanor's charter evidently arranged for the bastide to be governed by her representive (the governor), while the consuls represented the citizens. At least that was the practice at Monségur in the fourteenth century. Her charter was specific about the employment of lepers at Monségur, limiting their work to raising twenty sheep, one ram, a pig and six geese.

In front of the church runs the medieval rue Souley (Occitan for 'barn street'), where merchants sailing the Dropt would deposit their goods. The Gothic church itself, dedicated to Notre Dame, was begun shortly after the foundation of the bastide, and though over the centuries it has been modified, it has retained its ancient polygonal apse and the fourteenth-century colonnettes and arches of its south doorway.

Still preoccupied with problems in his English realms, Henry III's next bastide was founded in 1267 by his seneschal in Gascony, Jean de Lalinde, who named it after himself. The bastide of Lalinde withstood the ravages of the sixteenth-century wars of religion. Alas, in 1944 the retreating Nazis destroyed much of the town, as a reprisal for the activities of the Resistance in Périgord. All that remain today are a few vestiges of the ramparts, the pattern of the streets, and the thirteenth-century *porte Romane*. The gateway derives its name from the blocks of stone, cut by the Romans, out of which it is built. In the middle of the market place is a stone cross, set here in 1351. The *maison du Gouverneur* still stands, dating from 1597.

The site reveals the importance of trade for these English bastides.

Lalinde lies on the Roman road from Périgueux to Agen and on the major medieval trading route between La Rochelle and Montpellier. And just as merchants sailed the Dropt to Monségur, so they came to and went from Lalinde by way of the River Dordogne. A magnificent view of one of the two great loops of the river, the *cingle* de Trémolat (the other is the *cingle* de Montfort near Domme) opens up from the public garden of Lalinde, as the Dordogne flows down to Bergerac.

At several points this usually hospitable river became choppy here. A medieval legend attributed this turbulence to a malevolent beast, lurking in the waters with the intention of drowning and devouring mariners. As a precaution, before they sailed from Libourne the sailors would invoke the aid of the patron saint of Périgord, Saint Front, against this vicious reptile. From the terrace above the river you can still see across the waters the twelfth-century chapel of Saint-Front de Colubri, rising on its wooded ridge. Nowadays the current has been tamed by barrages, erected further up the river.

Still in the reign of Henry III, Prince Edward, heir to the English throne, followed his mother's example and in 1268 in *paréage* with the abbey of Pimbo founded the bastide of Pimbo on a hilltop site at what is now the south-easterly tip of the *département* of the Landes. Although the abbey, which Charlemagne had founded, was destroyed during the wars of religion, the bastide still cherishes the thirteenth-century Romanesque-Gothic church in which the monks once worshipped. Its sculpted porch depicts pineapples and interlinked persons. On either side are depicted the seven deadly sins. The rest of the bastide has preserved some sweet half-timbered houses.

Two years after founding Lalinde, with the aid of his seneschal Jean de Grailly, Edward set about creating the bastide of Libourne on the same river. Its strategic importance, enhanced by the fact that here the waters of the Dordogne are swollen by those of the Isle, had already been recognized by the foundation of a fortress town known as Fozera. Jean de Grailly did not finish the work of transforming Fozera into a bastide, and by letters patent of 24

November 1269, Prince Edward confided the task to Roger de Leyburn, from whom Libourne derives its name.

Its arcaded market square (place Abel-Surchamp) is still intact, at its centre an impressive eighteenth-century fountain. So is the fourteenth-century *porte du Pont* (known as the *porte Richard*), the sole survivor of eight which once pierced its walls. You can trace out nearby remnants of the ramparts. Though much restored, the delightful, Gothic town hall at one side of the market place dates essentially from the fifteenth century, boasting a monumental staircase and a hall with a superb chimney and a coffered ceiling. Here is preserved the 'hairy book', the sheepskin-covered *livre velu*, containing the charters granted to the bastide by the English kings.

Wool and wine were exported from Libourne from the thirteenth century, the former renowned as far away as Italy, the latter still renowned and including the celebrated red wines of Saint-Emilion, Pomeral and Fronsac and the whites of Entre-Deux-Mers and Graves de Vayres. In summer today its pedestrianized, chequerboard streets teem with visitors, who can inspect the former ramparts by way of the rue des Murs and visit the fourteenth-century church of Saint-Jean-Baptiste, which was once called Saint-Jean-de-Fozera and whose façade dates from 1853.

When Alphonse de Poitiers and Jeanne de Toulouse died in 1271, Henry III's precautions in protecting his French realms with bastides proved justified. In spite of the treaty of Paris, Philippe le Hardi held on to the Agenais, refusing to cede it to the English. The following year Henry III of England died, but his eldest son was away on crusade and did not return for his coronation until 1274. If his mother had paved the way in emulating French bastides, from now until his death in 1307 Edward I and his seneschals energetically built more to stem the advance of the Capetians into Plantagenet territory.

Because of Edward's delay in returning from the Holy Land, Lucas de Thenay, his father's seneschal in Guyenne, founded the first bastide of the new reign, on a rising site over the River Couze. Touchingly, the bastide of Beaumont-du-Périgord was laid out in the form of an H, in memory of Henry III. Wide and narrow streets cross each other at right angles. Of the fortifications the massive *porte de Luzier* still stands, the grooves for its portcullis now empty. If this portcullis was broached, invaders had to run along a narrow passageway to a second fortification.

Several arcades still surround the market place of Beaumont-du-

Périgord, and the bastide still welomes a fair here on the second Tuesday of the month. Apart from the *porte de Luzier*, what most reminds one of the perilous times in which the bastide was built is the fortified church of Saint Front. Built at the end of the thirteenth and the beginning of the fourteenth centuries, this is as much a fortress as a house of prayer. And yet its west façade contrives to be graceful, with an arched porch protected by a sculpted gallery and a frieze depicting a siren, a stag hunt, the four evangelists and the head of a king – perhaps representing Edward I, perhaps another tribute to Henry III.

Throughout his reign, which lasted from 1272 to 1307, Edward I incessantly founded bastides, altogether some thirty-five. Not all have remained intact, but some of those that have survived are superb and others almost as impressive. Among the latter is Labastide-d'Armagnac, set by the River Doulouze in the *département* of the Landes. Parts of the Landes are monotonous; but not this part. Labastide-d'Armagnac lies in a countryside of wooded hills, of pine trees and oaks, and of vines whose grapes make the Armagnac liqueur on which, along with tourism, the whole region as well as the bastide prospers.

Along with Count Bernard d'Armagnac, Edward I founded Labastide-d'Armagnac in 1284. Four streets converge on the exquisite central place Royale, which has arcades on three sides and houses sheltering covered walks. It is said that Henri IV modelled the place des Vosges in Paris on this square. On one side rises the Romanesque church of Our Lady, with a huge fifteenth-century tower, powerfully fortified, and under the nearby mairie is the medieval market hall. In narrow streets ancient houses dating from the thirteenth to the eighteenth centuries add their charm to the spot. Follow rue de la Chaussée to find the seventeenth-century communal washing place and further on by the River Douze the ruins of a huge fortified windmill dating from the fourteenth century.

A year later the king founded the bastide of Saint-Geours-d'Auribat, south-west of Labastide-d'Armagnac, to guard the reaches of the River Louts. In the next year he founded the bastide of Miramont-Sensacq not far from Pimbo, with the obvious aim of strengthening the defences of the Bas and Bahus valleys.

Far better preserved than these is the charming bastide of Vianne in the Lot-et-Garonne. In founding this bastide the English intended to counteract the influence of the nearby French bastide of Lavardac. Edward I entrusted his seneschal in Guyenne, Jean de Grailly, with the creation of Vianne in 1284, in conjunction with the lord of Montgaillard, Jourdain de l'Isle.

The name of the bastide acknowledges the source of Jourdain's wealth. His aunt on his mother's side, Vianne de Gontaud, managed to have both her marriages annulled – in the first instance by falsely convincing Pope Clement IV that her husband's father was also her godfather, in the second by persuading Pope Gregory X that the father of her second husband had never been baptized. Thus Vianne de Gontaud kept a grip on her rich dowry, retiring to Condom where she founded several convents for young noble girls and where she died on 21 February 1280, leaving her considerable wealth to her nephew Jourdain, son of her sister Indié. In gratitude, Jourdain named the bastide after his generous benefactor.

Apart from where its south-eastern wall angles itself to match the curve of the River Baïse, the bastide of Vianne is a perfect rectangle. Vianne has almost totally preserved its defensive system, the walls stretching some 1250 metres and pierced by four gateways topped by square towers, while another two round towers, with slits for arrows, strengthen the angles of the defences. The twelfth century Romanesque church of Saint Christopher is older than the bastide, built to serve the village of Villelongue which once occupied the site. Vianne has a little fountain and a market square, the place des Marroniers, approached by streets running at right angles to each other. Its church boasts a fourteenth-century façade, a little Romanesque apse, and splendid Romanesque capitals, carved with animals, foliage, a grinning head and an oddly-shaped human being. When the bastide was built, the church tower was fortified.

Jourdain de l'Isle retained some rights over the bastide. Whereas the right to sentence a malefactor to death was reserved for the king of England, for lesser offences Jourdain had the power to administer justice. Any fines or confiscations were to be divided between him and the king. Both Jourdain and the king had a bailiff to look after their affairs in Vianne, while the citizens had their elected consuls, charged to repair the fountains, the gates of the bastide and the streets. Six of them, chosen from among the inhabitants of the bastide and by faith Catholic, were elected for a year at the feast of Saint Michael.

Edward I also attracted citizens to Vianne by granting them a charter of customs on 19 April 1287. The original is lost, but a copy, made in 1310, survives. It exempts the citizens from paying taxes. They were given the right to sell their goods or houses without seeking permission of any overlord. As elsewhere, their daughters could be freely offered in marriage or freely enter convents. Everyone had the right to justice. If anyone died intestate, that person's goods were to be guarded for a year by two honest persons, in case an heir appeared. If no heir showed up, the goods were to revert to the king of England, after all debts had been duly paid.

Oaths were to be sworn before a clergyman and then respected. Quarrels should not be satisfied by duels but by proper process of law, with testimonies and other proofs. Anyone who threw rubbish in the streets was to be punished either by the representative of the king or by the consuls. Arsonists were to be particularly chastized. Murderers were to be tried by the king of England; anyone who insulted another should be fined two sols (i.e. *sous*); those who stole fruit, straw, grain or wood were to recompense their victims to the exact amount.

The rustic life of these bastides appears in the regulation that if anyone's bull, cow or other large animal trampled the gardens, vines or fields of another citizen, he should pay six deniers to the consuls, while if the damage were caused by a pig or sow, the fine was a mere three deniers (presumably because pigs and sows are harder to control than bulls and cows).

Thieves were punished at Vianne in intriguing ways. Anyone who stole goods worth up to two sols was to run through the streets of the bastide with the stolen property hanging from his or her neck, before paying a fine of five sols and restoring the goods to their rightful owner. If the stolen goods were worth more than five sols, the fine was sixty sols. And if anyone was hanged for stealing, the king of England was to be paid ten livres from his goods. Similarly, the goods of condemned murderers became the property of the king.

Fighting was especially discouraged. Hitting anyone with the hand or fist, or kicking another person, was punished with a fine of five sols, save where the blow had drawn blood, in which case the fine was raised to twenty sols. Blows with a sword, stick, stone or tile merited a fine of twenty sols, raised to sixty if blood had been drawn. Finally, men and women discovered committing adultery were given a choice: either they could pay a fine of 100 sols, or else they were to parade naked through the streets of the bastide.

Vianne's charter also dealt with the citizens' bread and butter. Anyone who wished could set up a bread oven, but had to pay the community twelve deniers a week for using it and selling the bread. Those who were found using false measures or weights were fined sixty sols. Market day was fixed as Tuesday, and any outsider wishing to sell goods there was to pay a rent.

To come upon a surviving bastide founded by Jean de Grailly (such as Vianne) is invariably to discover an aesthetic treat, an urban creation matching almost any other in the lands of the bastides. He founded Cadillac in the Gironde in 1280, again with the aim of both hemming in the French and promoting trade with England. Cadillac is sheltered by hills which overlook the meanders of the Garonne valley. Its fortifications are impressive, though they are not the work of the founder but date from the fourteenth century and were not finished until the eighteenth. One of the gates, the *porte de la Mer*, none-the-less bespeaks the seneschal's brilliance in choosing this site. Where today the boats of local fishermen dot the river, in the past larger (though only slightly larger) vessels, known as *gabares*, would set sail carrying goods and wine to be shipped across the sea from Bordeaux.

The masons who built Cadillac's fifteenth-century Gothic church took the opportunity of setting it against the defensive wall. Another road from the port reaches the second surviving gate of this bastide, the *porte de l'Horloge*, whose dome and lantern were added only in 1772.

In Monpazier Jean de Grailly has left us what many would consider the finest of all surviving bastides. Perfectly preserved and lying at the southern tip of the Dordogne on a plain above the River Dropt, it was founded on behalf of Edward 1 in 1284. Jean de Grailly intended his bastide to command the road from the south of France into Périgord. He obtained the land, a gentle hill known as Mont Pazerii, from Baron Pierre de Gontaud, the lord of Biron, the act of *paréage* being concluded between Pierre de Gontaud and Edward I on 7 January 1284. As elsewhere in the customs of the bastides of south-west France, jurisdiction over capital crimes was left in the hands of the monarch. At Monpazier rents and taxes were divided between the king and the Gontaud family. A later charter of customs decreed that six consuls and a royal bailiff should administer the bastide.

Former serfs, penniless peasants, men and women without homes or fleeing justice came to swear homage to the king and the baron in front of the *pal* set up in what was to be the market square of Monpazier. Each was allotted space for a house, a garden and cultivable land outside the bastide. They transformed an inhospitable land into an orchard, with chestnuts and walnuts, a countryside today blossoming with tobacco and strawberries.

These citizens built Monpazier in less than six years. Initially work was hampered by a severe drought, which dried up the local streams and the Dropt. When Edward I himself arrived to inspect his lands on 6 November 1286, he found the fortifications scarcely begun and insisted that the consuls speed up the work. They took the king at his word and completed them three years later.

Gates, towers and parts of the walls survive. The plan of the bastide is perfectly regular. The market square is a gem, all its houses built in the thirteenth century, all of them of the same dimensions, namely 8 metres wide and 20 metres deep. Balconies and Gothic arcades have been added to enliven some of their pale ochre walls. Gothic arcades surround the square, and are also set at angles at each corner. Little passages, only 30 centimetres in width and known *andronnes*, separate the houses to allow water and filth to escape and also as a precaution against the spread of fire.

To one side of the market square rises the exceptionally beautiful sixteenth-century market hall. The fretted woodwork of its pantiled roof is supported on chestnut beams rising from stone supports. Here, as for example at Villefranche-du-Périgord, you can see three ancient measures, bucket shaped and swung on hinges, which made sure that the citizens did not cheat each other when selling grain. At one corner of the square is the bastide's well.

On the way to the parish church of Saint Dominic you pass the house of the canons, three-storeyed with Gothic bays, which also served for collecting tithes. Almost opposite, the church itself is in origin contemporary with the foundation of the bastide, begun in 1289 though over the next two centuries it was modified, its apse and surrounds added in the fifteenth century, the choir finally completed in 1506. Its Gothic arches remain satisfyingly simple, growing more delicate as you walk east. Those of the choir rise from intricately carved capitals. Naturally in a bastide, the church is fortified, its square tower dating from the sixteenth century. The finely sculpted tympanum dates from the sixteenth and seventeenth centuries. Over its doorway you can still read the inscription added by the Jacobins of Monpazier at the time of the French Revolution: 'The people of France recognize the existence of the Supreme Being and the immortality of the soul.'

When Edward II succeeded his father in 1307 he had another twenty years to live and devoted almost as much of his energies to founding bastides as had Edward I. In 1313 his seneschal Amaury de Créon built for him the eponymous Créon in the Gironde, its central place de la Prévôté still surrounded by arcaded houses, its streets running off at right angles, its parish church dating from the fifteenth century. As we have already noted, it soon became a staging-post on the major route from Paris to the shrine of Saint James the Great at Santiago de Compostela.

Five years later Edward II founded Geaune-en-Tursan in the same *département*, in *paréage* with the lord of Castelnau-Tursan which lies a few kilometres north. At Geaune, which is now the capital of the quiet, rural region of Tursan, you can still explore the central square, arcaded on three sides. In 1880 its citizens foolishly demolished the old market hall, but the west side of the square still has delightful wooden houses, while others are built of brick and stone. As for the fifteenth-century church of Saint John the Baptist, its huge, fortified belfry dates from 1452, beneath which the entrance to the church opens under an ogival vault.

This is the region of such bastides as Pimbo and Miramont-Sensacq, founded in the previous reign. Evidently Edward II still felt threatened in this part of his domains. In 1315 we find him founding Sarron, due east of Miramont-Sensacq. Little remains of his bastide, save for a Romanesque church. Further north he strengthened the defences beside the River Bahus by founding Buanes, where you can still make out traces of the bastide and admire the elegant belfry-wall of the fourteenth-century parish church. Smitten with the penchant of his predecessors for naming bastides after great foreign cities, in 1322 he founded Grenade-sur-l'Adour, to command the River Adour north of Sarron. Along with several medieval houses, Grenade-sur-l'Adour has preserved the central, arcaded square of a medieval bastide. Obsessed with defending the river beside which it stands, Edward II also founded the bastide of Saint-Maurice-sur-l'Adour a few kilometres further west.

In the Lot-et-Garonne he strengthened his father's work by founding the bastide of Durance in 1320, in *paréage* with the Premonstratensian monks of the abbey of Castelle-sur-l'Adour. Their thirteenth-century abbey church, just north of the bastide, lies today in ruins, but Durance has survived. Its plan is a trifle higgledy-piggledy for a bastide, though the streets do run more or less at right angles to each other. Of Edward II's fortifications, the south gate has withstood the depredations of the centuries, surmounted by a square tower and protected with narrow loopholes through which defenders could shoot arrows at their enemies. Walking through the gate you shortly reach the spacious central square, to the left of which rises a stern parish church, built in the fourteenth century. Beyond the church is another fortified gateway and a stretch of the ancient wall.

Under Edward III the Hundred Years War finally broke out. The spark of Saint-Sardos lit kindling that had been amassed for over a decade. In 1316, King Louis X of France had died leaving only a daughter and no male heir. Accordingly his brothers Philippe and Charles successively ascended the throne. When Charles died in 1328, he too left no male heir. His cousin Philippe of Valois claimed the throne.

Edward III, however, was a grandson of Philippe le Bel on his mother's side. His claim to the French throne was that although no woman could occupy it, she could transmit that right to her male children. In support of this claim Edward declared war against France in 1337. Not surprisingly, he had little scope for building in the land he was invading, and founded few bastides. He had determined to found Saint-Pierre-de-Londres in the Lot-et-Garonne ten years before he declared war. All that remains today is the the belfry and the Romanesque porch of its church. Over the low tympanum, surrounded nowadays by briars and weeds, you can still make out a carved relief of Jesus in majesty, surrounded by the symbols of the four evangelists. Edward III also paid his dues in defending the lower parts of the Landes by founding the bastide of Momuy in 1341, but scarcely anything looking like a bastide now survives there.

In a previous skirmish, beginning in 1294 and continuing intermittently for nine years, the English had already taken up arms to defend their territories, coming up against these newly founded defensive towns known as bastides. In December 1282, English troops had disembarked at the mouth of the Garonne, and within a month were masters of the region around Sordes. By 1294 the French were fighting back. At Bonnegarde, a bastide in the Landes founded by Edward I in 1279, a garrison commanded by Robert d'Artois was in possession of the town when the earl of Lincoln attacked with upwards of 5000 foot soldiers and 700 horsemen. To his surprise the French army was ready for him and he was obliged to withdraw with his troops to Peyrehorade.

At Vianne the English suffered a similar setback. The lord of Mont-cassin was mortally wounded defending this bastide. Elated at the news, the English renewed their attack. The citizens dressed the corpse of their lord in his armour and hoisted it on to the battlements, at which the dumbfounded English lifted the siege.

The English did not remain dumbfounded. They took Vianne in 1340, as well as nearby Damazan and Villefranche-du-Queyran. Throughout the war, these bastides repeatedly changed hands. Vianne was again captured by the English in 1437. Shortly afterwards the armies of the French king took it back. Two years later the earl of Huntingdon arrived with a force of 1500 men, capturing not only Vianne but also the neighbouring bastides of Durance and Lavardac. The Agenais was completely liberated from the English only in 1442.

Once thought impregnable, many bastides clearly proved as vulnerable as other towns and cities throughout France. Domme, on its supposedly unassailable height, was in the hands of the English in 1346. The following year the French took it back, and the consuls and citizens seized the opportunity of asking Philippe le Hardi to confirm their charter of rights. Those of its citizens who had espoused the English cause were hanged in the market square. An English army arrived at the foot of its rock in 1369, failed to take the bastide and withdrew. In 1421 the same thing happened again.

The Black Prince had landed at Bordeaux in 1355, setting out from there to ravage the countryside, using his notorious technique known as the *chevauché*, in which knights on horseback made devastating raids giving no quarter and showing no mercy. His brilliance as a soldier enabled the English to win the battle of Poitiers in 1356 and capture the French king Jean le Bon; Edward III gave the duchy of Guyenne to the Black Prince and for a time his might prevailed throughout Aquitaine.

Other bastides besides Domme suffered the terrors of this war. In the Gironde, Monségur was besieged by the English, while SainteFoylaGrande was captured by them and became French again only at the end of the war in 1453. In some cases the English were simply taking back from the French what had originally been theirs. The still fortified bastide of SauveterredeGuyenne in the Gironde had been founded by Edward I in 1281. In 1386, Charles VI claimed it for the French crown. The English took it back in 1420, and SauveterredeGuyenne became finally and definitively French only in 1451.

Surprisingly, these ravages left many a bastide unspoilt. At SauveterredeGuyenne not only are the four medieval gates of the town still intact in the fortifications; so are many medieval houses, the communal wash house and fountain, the bastide's windmills and the arcaded market square.

One powerful founder of bastides managed to keep clear of the whole terrible war. In the late fourteenth century Viscount Gaston Fébus of Béarn ruled the region where we have already explored the bastide of Sorde-l'Abbaye. Ruler of Foix-Béarn from the age of twelve (for the first two years under the tutelage of his mother Elénor de Comminges), Gaston III de Foix changed his name in 1358 to Fébus (from Phoebus, the Greek word for radiant which was used as the name of the sun-god), in part because of his own golden hair, in part because of his vanity, and in part because he believed the spreading rays of the sun were matched by his expanding realms. On the front of his châteaux he exulted in seeing engraved the words FEBUS ME FE.

Gaston Fébus had married Agnes of Navarre in 1348. He seems to have been both brilliant and slightly insane. One of his passions was hunting, about which he wrote a treatise, and in 1391 he died at the age of sixty indulging this passion (some say poisoned, others of a heart attack). A patron of troubadours, a fierce warrior and an able administrator of his province, he also assassinated his brother in a fit of rage and in another display of anger killed his only son, whom he supposed to have been implicated in a plot against him instigated by Gaston's wife. He then retired to his château at Pau and wrote a book of prayers to expiate the murder.

Gaston also hated the count of Armagnac, his powerful neighbour who had taken the side of the French king Jean II le Bon in the Hundred Years War. To protect himself against his enemy's allies, Gaston fortified Labastide-Villefranche (which Marguérite de Béarn had founded in 1292), 50 kilometres from Bayonne, where the English had installed themselves.

This enmity caused him not only to strengthen his own frontiers but also to prosecute a successful war against the count in 1362. Among Gaston's possessions was the bastide of Launac, which lies north-west of Toulouse. It had been founded in the late thirteenth century by a baron of Launac, who gave its citizens a charter in 1290 and another in 1297. In 1362, Gaston found it a fitting spot to imprison the counts of Armagnac and Comminges.

Gaston Fébus owned other bastides in this region, such as Palaminy, which lies on the left bank of the Garonne, south-west of Toulouse. Further south-west he made Mauvezin one of his strongholds, and here his fortress still stands, the tall, square and machicolated keep rising above the power-fully, buttressed rectangular walls. And to protect his frontier with Bigorre in 1335 he founded the bastide of Lestelle-Bétharram, whose streets still run at right angles to each other, converging on the central market square.

In founding his own bastides, Gaston Fébus was not averse to the megalomanic habit of calling them after the great cities of Europe. In the *département* of the Pyrénées-Atlantiques his lieutenant-general Bertrand de Puyols founded Bruges (now Bruges-Capbis-Mifaget) in the late 1350s, giving the citizens their charter around 1360. On Gaston's behalf Bertrand had made an expedition to Prussia, passing through Bruges on the way. Within sight of the Pyrenees, Bruges-Capbis-Mifaget commands the rivers Beez and Landistou. The vast arcaded market square is intact, as are several watermills and the Gothic parish church.

The Hundred Years War came to an end in 1453 at Castillon, not far from the bastide of Libourne, after the town had been besieged by the French under King Charles VII. The 75-year old John Talbot, earl of Shrewsbury and Watford, marched from Bordeaux in an attempt to lift the siege. In a disastrous error, he decided that his troops should fight with their backs to the river, making any retreat impossible. Talbot's own horse was brought down, trapping the earl beneath it, and a French archer killed him with an axe. As the rest of his army tried to flee, many of the soldiers were also slaughtered. A few months later Charles VII was master of all of Gascony and Guyenne. After the battle of Castillon the town proudly added the words 'la-Bataille' to its name.

If many bastides were left surprisingly intact by the Hundred Years War, the sixteenth-century wars of religion did more damage. Protestants were particularly keen on destroying the symbols of the papacy and some-times included churches among them. The bastide of Puymirol founded by Raymond VI of Toulouse once boasted two churches, one dedicated to Saturnin (or Sernin), the patron saint of Toulouse, the other to Notre-Dame-du-Grand-Castel. Saint Sernin had stood here longer than the bas-tide, for this hill of Puymirol dominates an important crossroads and medi-eval travellers needed to invoke the protection of a reputed saint. In 1578 the Protestants took control of the bastide and destroyed both churches, save for the belfry of Notre-Dame. After the Edict of Nantes, which Henri IV promulgated in 1598, giving Protestants and Catholics equal rights to toleration throughout France, Bishop Nicholas de Villars decided to rebuild a church at Puymirol which was to be used by both religious communities. Work began in 1600, to be finished in 1640. On the east and north walls the architect inscribed in Latin the sentences 'de Lereberette made me in 1640', and 'this building, pulled down by the sectarianism of the enemies of the Catholic faith, was rebuilt thanks to the charity of the judges, consuls and notables in the year 1640'.

Solomniac in the *département* of the Gers is a bastide which fared less well during the wars of religion. The bastide still preserves its streets set at right angles to each other, its market hall rises from stone pillars, and the bastide boasts delightful half-timbered houses. The church, ruined by the Protestants in 1580 and restored in the seventeenth and eighteenth centuries, stands apart from the main square, near the wash house. But Solomniac is a shadow of its former self.

Domme provides a more entertaining example of the vicissitudes of the wars of religion. In 1572 the Protestant captain Geoffroy de Vivans attempted to take the bastide, but retired wounded. On 4 June he managed to discover a traitor in the bastide, who promised to open the gates and let in the Protestant troops. Then the traitor had second thoughts, revealed the plot to the governor, and once again Geoffroy de Vivans retired. Undeterred, he decided that it was possible to scale the 150-metre-high cliff overlooking the Dordogne, which the citizens of Domme had left unprotected, believing that no one could climb it. On 25 October 1588, the Protestants managed the feat and Domme was taken. Geoffroy burned down most of the church and then descended to the nearby village of Cénac, where he destroyed all but the eastern end of the priory.

Troubles did not cease with the ending of the wars of religion. In the late sixteenth and throughout the seventeenth centuries many French peasants were almost continually in revolt, particularly in Périgord. They were known as *croquants*, a word that signified those who grind their teeth together – since, presumably, they had precious little else to grind between them. Their staple food was chestnuts, occasionally supplemented with a piece of hard bread rubbed with garlic.

The novelist Eugène Le Roy, whom we have already spotted in Domme, evoked their miserable fate. His masterpiece is *Jacquou le Croquant*, the tale of another tooth-grinder (Jacquou is the patois version of Jacques).

Until orphaned at the age of nine, Jacquou lives with his parents in the Dordogne, scratching a living in the deep Barade forest along with charcoal-burners, tinsmiths, goatherds and the like. When the boy and his mother peer into a château's kitchen on Christmas Eve, Eugène Le Roy contrasts the difference in diet between the great ones in the châteaux of the Dordogne and such wretched peasant children as Jacquou.

On the immense fire-dogs of forged iron burned a huge fire of six-foot logs, before which was roasting a fat turkey-cock, stuffed with truffles, which smelled deliciously. One of the two grills was loaded with puddings, the other with pigs' trotters, ready to be placed on the spit which a scullery-maid was turning in the corner of the chimney. On this table, too, stood slices of cold meat and pâtés in their golden crusts.

When the two return to their miserable hovel, Jacquou's mother gives him for supper a corn ball, or *mique*. 'As I was eating this *mique*, kneaded with water, cooked with cabbage leaves, without even a scrap of lard in it, and completely cold,' he recalls, 'I was thinking about all those good things that I had glimpsed in the kitchen of the château, and I do not deny that it made the *mique* seem a poor affair – as indeed it was.'

The *croquants* rioted in 1594. Their struggle, in the words of the historian Emmanuel Le Roy Ladurie, was 'against the nobility who treated rustics like slaves . . . and against the royalist rogues who had stolen the oxen and raped the girls.' It involved 'a refusal, if possible, to pay tithes, tailles [local taxes] and rents'. The revolt was 'a defence of the country folk against the urban bourgeoisie, who set high prices on their wares and demanded high rents for fields and farms purchased for a song'.

The 1590s were years of famine, stoking up resentments amongst the poor. Domme was a hotbed of the *croquants*, who were subdued only by the presence of royal troops. In 1594 hundreds of *croquants* assembled at Monpazier, before disappearing into the forests. They revolted again in 1597 and dissension spread throughout Aquitaine.

For forty years peasant despair simmered beneath the surface of Périgord. In 1637 the *croquants* mounted their greatest threat to the stability of south-west France. Led by a weaver from Capdrot named Buffarot, 8000 armed peasants pillaged châteaux throughout the Dordogne. The duke of Epernon, governor of Guyenne, charged Pierre de Molinier, a leading citizen of Monpazier, to put down the rebellion. He succeeded, and on 6 August 1637, Buffarot was broken on the wheel in Monpazier's market square. One of the annual fairs granted in Monpazier's charter is still held on 6 August.

Uncannily, in all these vicissitudes the bastides managed to retain their unique beauty. Puymirol, despite losing a church, remains exquisite. Trie-sur-Baïse in the Hautes-Pyrénées, founded by Jean de Trie, seneschal of Toulouse, in 1322, was repeatedly attacked during the Hundred Years War and part of it was set on fire in 1569 during the religious wars, yet its fortifications, its two round defensive towers, its powerful square gateway-tower, its huge central square, its fifteenth-century church and its chequer-board streets are still intact.

To explore other examples, in 1439 the count of Huntingdon disembarked at Bordeaux with 15,000 men and proceeded to take the bastides of Francescas and Lamontjoie. The first had been founded by Edward I in 1286, in *paréage* with the monks of Condom. In 1439 its captors declined to destroy the thirteenth-century church, which now has a hammerbeam roof, or ravage the arcaded, irregular market square. They even left standing a house belonging to a friend of their enemy Joan of Arc, who had been recently burned at the stake.

At nearby Lamontjoie they came upon a bastide that had repeatedly changed hands throughout the Hundred Years War. The English annexed it in 1317, and the French took it back. Yet the pattern of its streets remains as when it was first built, and arcades still add charm to its market square. Even more remarkable in my view is that no one thought to extirpate the relics of Saint Louis himself, five fragments of his hand, which are still enshrined in Lamontjoie's parish church. As a bonus, Philippe le Bel had given the bastide these sacred remains when he granted Lamontjoie its charter in 1299.

Seemingly, men and women in the past were willing to slaughter each other but unwilling to destroy their architectural, urban patrimony. At Rabastens-de-Bigorre, for example, a bastide founded in the Hautes-Pyrénées in 1306 by the seneschal Guillaume de Rabastens, numerous Protestants were massacred by the Catholics in 1570. No one pillaged Rabastens-de-Bigorre. The spot still displays all the classic elements of a bastide: rectilinear streets; a fourteenth-century brick and sandstone church; a huge market square with a covered market hall and a fountain.

Not all bastides were so sumptuous or founded by such great ones. In the twelfth century a dozen or so humbler ones were created in what is now the *département* of the Lot. The first, Labastide-du-Vert, was founded by Raymond Alric shortly after the Albigensian crusade. At the last census its population was 167. Next came Bretenoux, founded as Villafranca by the seigneur of Castelnau in 1277, followed twenty years later by Montcabrier, which is set on a defensive hillock in the lush valley of the Thèze.

Compared with the great bastides these humbler ones present a different allure. Their fragility makes it even more remarkable that so many of them have remained remarkably intact. The arcades of sleepy Montcabrier have been transformed into shops and homes for its inhabitants, who number a mere 380. This bastide supports not a single bar. But traces of its former glory remain: a delicately carved Renaissance window; a house with a turret; and above all its powerfully fortified church, which boasts a superb west end with a Gothic rose window and doorway, a baroque altarpiece and a belfry capable of bearing five bells. (These days it carries only three.)

To explore the neighbourhood of Montcabrier makes it seem all the more remarkable that such an apparently fragile creation should have sur-vived as the refuge of free citizens (whose franchises were granted by Philip le Bel in 1304). The bastide is surrounded by what were once the citadels of feudal baronies. A few kilometres north east is Montcléra, which was a subordinate fief of the powerful Guerre family. The château which kept their subjects in order can still be seen there. At the other side of Montcabrier, seven kilometres south east, is Puy-l'Evêque, which took its name from the bishop who reconquered the town from the Cathars. Today it is dominated by a powerful fortress, and yet these ambitious bishops failed to take control of little Montcabrier, as did the lords of the fortress of Bonaguil, scarcely twenty kilometres south west. In fact, the citizens of the minuscule bastide spent most of the Middle Ages defending themselves against Pestillac, the minor barony at the other side of the valley. They survived.

Their survival is a testimony to the genius of those who created these new towns, enclaves of security in dangerous times, homes of free men and women intent on prospering whatever might happen. In 1361, shortly after the Black Death had decimated Europe, Petrarch was sent to congratulate the French king on his liberation from the English. The poet has left us a telling insight into the condition of France at that time. 'Everywhere was solitude, desolation and misery,' he wrote. 'Everywhere you see the fatal footprints of the English and the hateful scars still bleeding from their swords.'

He added: 'Fields are deserted, houses ruined and empty, except in the walled towns.' Those walled towns were the bastides.

Down the
Centuries

In the early fourteenth century King Philippe V of France decided to assert his authority more strongly in the Hautes-Pyrénées, intent on curbing the agitation of the little feudal lords in the region. Determined to foster a group of citizens loyal to the French monarchy, he did so by founding two bastides, beginning with Galan whose charter was granted in 1319, two years after the king's accession to the throne. Galan dominates two tributaries of the River Baïse, namely the Baïsole and the Petite Baïse. In 1322 the king instructed the seneschal of Toulouse, Jean de Trie, to found a bastide beside the River Baïse itself. So Trie-sur-Baïse was born.

The birth of a bastide was a lengthy and ceremonial affair. At Trie-sur-Baïse the bastide was conceived with the contract of *paréage*, signed in the presence of a notary by all parties setting up the new town, and supervised by the seneschal of the king in whose interest the bastide was being founded.

For Trie-sur-Baïse the ceremony took place on 11 January 1322 in the château of Duffort. Jean de Trie supervised the whole proceedings. The preamble to the act of *paréage* declares that the seigneurs who signed it, along with the abbot representing the monastery of Escaladieu relinquished their right to the land but not their right to their feudal dues. They pledged their oath to protect the king and his officers, as well as their goods, and to defend the future bastide, whose consuls and inhabitants would do the same. The founders and the monks agreed by this contract to nominate syndics, who, along with the officers of the king, would fix the limits of the bastide and the lands around it which its future citizens would till. Philippe de Verdier, a judge of Rivière-Verdun, signed on behalf of the king; the seigneurs of Montbardon-Duffort and Puydarnieux, Bernard de Manas and Gérard d'Esparros, also signed, as did Roger de Mauléon, abbot of Escaladieu.

The following year the king was dead, but his bastide emerged into life. As often with other bastides, a long stake or *pal* was raised at the spot destined to become the market square, a ceremony known in the medieval documents as the *fixatio pali*. Spaces were reserved for the church and its cemetery. Then, supervised by the officers of the sovereign, surveyors marked out the street pattern and the parcels of land allotted for the houses and vegetable gardens of the future inhabitants, for these were to be garden cities. Finally, outside what would become the still-surviving fortifications of Trie-sur-Baïse, further plots of land were marked out for future clearance and cultivation.

Inside any bastide by the fourteenth century, those who drew up the pattern of its streets at its foundation traditionally divided them into four sorts. The main axis of a bastide was traversed (and still is) by what are known as *rues charretières* (or *carreyras* in Occitan), which literally means 'roads for carters'. These were the thoroughfares, usually around 8 metres wide, through which horses and carts could easily pass (and which nowadays are often clogged up with the parked cars of the visitors who throng the bastides).

Often the *rues charretières* were given names signifying their particular importance. At Monflanquin in the Lot-et-Garonne, for instance, the two *rues charretières* are dubbed rue Sainte-Marie and rue Saint-Pierre, after Jesus's mother and his chief disciple. They run on either side of the place des Arcades, which here is 55 metres long and 25 metres wide.

Nearly as important and usually a couple of metres narrower were the streets which crossed these at right angles, in the case of Monflanquin rue des Arcades, rue de l'Union and rue de la Paix. Narrower streets, which could scarcely allow even one-way traffic, are often known as *carrérots* (or, since all the bastides are situated in the Languedoc, in Occitan *carrérous*). Still taking Monflanquin as an example, you can stroll here along the carrérot des Augustins, the carrérot des Crugiers, the carrérot Bernard Palissy or the carrérot des Cabannes (which, for some melancholy reason I have not discovered, is also called rue Sans Joie, the joyless street). They are flanked by houses built of roughly hewn stones, their doorways with pointed and round arches. Lastly came openings that no one was expected to walk along, the *androses*, where rainfall drained away, taking with it dirty water from the houses and the effluent of the latrines.

In a medieval bastide a *carrérot* served the same purpose as a twentieth century pedestrianized street. At Monflanquin, where the medieval pattern of the bastides and its streets has been scrupulously restored, the carrérot des Augustins enabled the citizens to walk as far as an Augustinian convent, of which we first hear in 1333 when Anne de Grailly left the monks ten livres in her will. The convent is no more, destroyed at the time of the Reformation.

In subsequent centuries what survived of its chapel was restored as Monflanquin's Protestant church, and what remained of the conventual buildings nowadays serves as an old people's home, an arch joining the two together across the carrérot des Augustins. This is a vestige of one of those little bridges, the *pontets*, which are one of the most charming features of this bastide. Delicately built of wood and brick, sometimes held up with beams, at other times borne on stone arches, these *pontets* constitute private overhead passages joining two houses across a *carrérot*, Monflanquin's rustic equiva-lents of the Bridge of Sighs in Venice.

Carrérot des Augustins still runs to a church, Monflanquin's splendid parish church of Notre-Dame. It once shaded the bastide's cemetery, but in 1820 this was transferred below the town, not so much for health reasons as to provide a place for parking horses and carts inside the town. The Gothic church of Notre-Dame was begun in the late thirteenth century. Its apse abuts on to the former ramparts.

In past times this church possessed some seven chapels as well as a sacristy, but some of these have disappeared, partly incorporated, as you can see from the style of architecture, in the houses on the south side of the church. This house of God was enlarged in the eighteenth century and again in the mid-nineteenth. You can make out where the round windows of the eighteenth-century church have been filled in, below a cornice clearly mark-ing where building stopped. Nineteenth-century Monflanquin added the ogival windows above this cornice and also finished the vaulting inside. The porch dates from the very beginning of the building, but surprisingly the battlemented façade and the Toulouse-type towers were added only after 1923, when lightning damaged the earlier, far less impressive façade.

New citizens had to be found to build these churches, to erect houses alongside the streets and create the market halls and fortifications of the medieval bastides. Once the act of *paréage* had been concluded, it was vital for the sovereigns and lords who founded these spots to issue a charter of customs,

defining the rights, privileges and duties of future citizens, with the express
purpose of tempting them to set up their homes in the new town. Monflanquin's first charter was signed at Vincennes by Alphonse de Poitiers in 1256,
a mere four years after he had obtained the site for his bastide, and on
Alphonse's behalf the seneschal of the Agenais speedily promulgated it in the
region. However much they differ in details, the charters of all the bastides
concern themselves with the same four themes: penal laws; civil liberties;
political liberties; and economic duties and rights.

Few bastides found difficulty in attracting inhabitants. In the century
before Philippe V founded Trie-sur-Baïse, the population of France had
unexpectedly grown. During the eleventh and early twelfth centuries a
small rise in the children of the families of Aquitaine and Gascony had
been easily absorbed in the new *castelnaux* and *sauvetés* of the two regions. But
the birth rate now suddenly accelerated, and these were inadequate to cater for
the newly swollen population. France boasted sixteen million inhabitants in
1226. A hundred years later the population was some one and a half millions
more (at a time when that of England was a mere two and a half millions). By
the mid-fourteenth century more than twenty million people were living in
the land. That is to say that between 1226 and the foundation of Trie-sur-
Baïse, the population of France had increased by twenty-five per cent.

Desperate for work, some of this huge number of people began to
emigrate to Spain, where such new cities as Estella and Logroño welcomed
them. Others moved from the north to Aquitaine, seizing the chance to
labour in the vineyards around Bordeaux and upper Gascony. Périgueux,
capital of the Périgord, rapidly acquired new suburbs, as did Bordeaux itself
and Bayonne.

We can best see the effect of this burgeoning population first in Bordeaux and then in the bastides. To accommodate immigrants from northern
France and the peasants who flocked to the city from the surrounding regions,
medieval Bordeaux built houses so tall that the narrow streets were perma-

nently dark. Candlemakers, builders, woodworkers, weavers, glassmakers, cabinet-makers and inevitably lawyers flourished in the city, as did the religious – monks, nuns and secular clergy whose churches catered not only for pilgrims to Santiago de Compostela but also for the various workers' guilds, Saint Jacques caring for the butchers, Saint Christophe for the porters and so on. Criminals also flourished, and the chief gibbet opposite the Ombrière palace was kept busy. Others died excommunicated, such as Pierre Colom, who was censured by the church for having the temerity to build a windmill up-wind of that of the archbishop.

In earlier times Bordeaux, like many of the bastides, was encircled with forests. In a burst of energy similar to that displayed in the new towns of the south-west, the forests were cleared, land was cultivated and vines planted, in those days powerful shoots which grew to the height of a man. Since for some 300 years Bordeaux was under English rule, the export of wine to England was indisputably its most profitable enterprise, and one which guaranteed some prosperity to the hinterland where the superfluous population of the rest of France increasingly sought homes. The region prospered particularly when rival sovereigns were occupied otherwise than in fighting each other, when for instance Saint Louis IX of France was crusading against the Muslims and the barons of England were preoccupying Henry III.

Wars provoked the desire for safe strongholds. Opposite Villeneuve-sur-Lot rises the much older town of Pujols. By the twelfth century it was ringed with three walls (some parts of the middle one still intact), but these could not prevent the destruction of its château during the Albigensian crusade. The monks and citizens of Pujols fled, taking refuge in the new town of Villeneuve-sur-Lot.

A fine defensive site, usually on a hill, was frequently attractive enough to tempt the founders, even if the contours made life less easy for those who had to build the bastide and later live in it. Domme is a case in point, its new citizens dismayed to learn that one of their allotted tasks was to build walls around the difficult spur. They also had a long way to trudge to their fields outside the town. Though Domme later prospered and the fields below its walls became lush, initially its inhabitants were so badly off that in 1310 Philippe le Bel charged his seneschal to enquire into their state. He reported back that some of them had no choice but to beg beside the streets.

At Monflanquin similar problems arose over fortifying the new town.

After the death of Alphonse de Poitiers and his wife Jeanne, by the arrangement which Louis IX had made with the English the bastide passed into
the hands of Edward I. He inherited a quarrel about who was to pay for the
ramparts, the king or the consuls. In 1282 his seneschal Jean de Grailly was
dispatched to resolve the matter and came up with a compromise. The
consuls should pay for the walls, while the fortified gateways – eight of them
– became the responsibility of the English king. Monflanquin's defences
were duly built, to be demolished on the orders of Richelieu in the late
1620s, their pattern now traced by the oval-shaped boulevards of the bastide. Curiously enough, some of the stones of these ramparts, demolished on
the orders of a Catholic servant of a Catholic king, were used to transform
the Augustinian chapel into the Protestant church at Monflanquin.

The builders of other bastides coped with irregular sites with less
dissension. Hastingues in the Landes, a foundation of Edward I of
England which took its name from his seneschal John de Hastings, is set on
another hilly site, this one dominating the valley of the Gaves Réunis not far
from their confluence with the River Adour. Notwithstanding the difficulties of the site, from the arcaded and regular market square the main
street, 6 metres wide, runs in a perfectly straight line to the main gateway of
the town.

Sauveterre-de-Guyenne and Monségur in the *département* of the
Gironde are two other bastides perched defensively on hills, the former still
defended by four medieval gates (its walls were demolished in the nineteenth
century), the latter's picturesque streets surrounded by vestiges of the old
fortifications. At Sauveterre-de-Guyenne the demands of the site forced the
founders to build the market square on a slope. Monflanquin rises above the
River Lède on an 181-metre hill which Guillaume Amanieu, lord of Calviac, sold to Alphonse de Poitiers in 1252.

The Lot-et-Garonne boasts many more bastides set on hilltop sites,
often identifiable as such simply by their names. Monclar d'Agenais, for

instance, is an exact contemporary of Monflanquin, also founded by Alphonse de Poitiers, and set on a 187-metre height commanding the valleys of the Lot and the Tolzat. Its place du Marché is arcaded, its late Gothic parish church dating from the turn of the fifteenth and sixteenth centuries. Montpezat is a third, which we have already explored, this bastide overlooking not only the Lot but also the River Bausse. A fourth is Monsempron-Libos, a bastide founded in 1305 by Edward 1 of England 116 metres above the confluence of the Lot and the Lémance.

Even when the two countries of England and France were not in conflict, life in south-west France remained perilous. The whole region was roamed by brigands. Froissart in his chronicles leaves us in little doubt of the serious threat they posed. Former soldiers, cut-throats, common criminals, they gathered together in organized bands to terrorize various parts of the coutryside, concentrating particularly on the forested regions of Périgord and the Agenais.

Several bastides deliberately set out to be oases where men and women could take refuge from these malefactors. In the Lot-et-Garonne are two whose charters specifically mention brigands. Unable to cope with such bandits, the abbot of Cadouin and Arnaud de Mons, lord of Lanquais, begged Alphonse de Poitiers to found a bastide at Castillonnès whose charter specifically deals with the problem. 'For the honour of God and the glorious Virgin Mary, her mother and our mother the Church,' runs one of its clauses,

> desiring that the virtue of peace and concord should reign over the said places, a town shall be built, since the said forest is situated in the midst of a perverse people, having long time been deserted save for thieves, brigands and evil subjects who have made their abode there, so that farmers and people of goodwill dare not live there and the arms of the lords cannot stretch out with enough strength to maintain peace and defend the country against criminals and persons of evil intent.

In fact it was not the French but the king of England who finally encircled Castillonnès with walls in the fourteenth century. Vestiges of the walls still remain, including fourteenth-century fortified gates, through which you reach the arcaded market square.

The foundation charter of Lamontjoie in the same *département* is equally emphatic, proclaiming that Gérard de Cépois, sensechal of Philippe le Bel in the Agenais, well aware that scoundrels were in the habit of molesting innocent persons, inflicting on them various cruelties and acts of violence, planned to build a bastide which would be strong enough to banish such wrongdoers from the territory. 'So that the inhabitants of this place should enjoy forever tranquillity and peace,' Gérard continued, 'on the part of the said king we have decided to found in this place a bastide named Lamontjoie de Saint Louis, after having invoked the assistance of God the Father, God the Son and God the Holy Ghost.'

Alongside these strategic, political and defensive reasons for creating bastides, simple economic considerations also played their part. However disastrous they had proved, the crusades had opened up trading routes, and bastides set beside rivers were poised to exploit them. Aiguillon today happily lives in part off tourism; but when it received its charter from Philippe le Bel in 1295 its importance lay in its site, at the confluence of the Lot and the Garonne where both were navigable. Now its status as a bastide is revealed only by the spacious central square and the chequerboard pattern of its streets. Its ramparts overlook the railway and beyond it fertile fields. The aspect of Aiguillon today is peaceful, but in the turbulent Middle Ages its citizens had little mercy for captured and condemned brigands, exposing their executed bodies at the local crossroads for all to see.

In promoting commerce and prosperity the fairs and markets were of supreme importance, and every charter of customs granted these to its particu-lar bastide. Citizens of the bastides could trade in the market free of charge, but strangers wishing to join in were taxed. At Labastide-Castel-Amouroux the tax was one denier for every cow or pig over the age of one which the stranger sold; two deniers for a donkey; a denier for a large measure of salt; two for a bundle of leather, for ironmongery or fleeces; and two for selling shoes, fire-dogs; boilers, cauldrons or hoes. The charter of the bastide of Montgéard in the Haute-Garonne prescribed that any stranger who sold a bull, a pig or a donkey at the fair should pay the king a twelfth of a sou, and those who sold wax should pay him half a denier.

Fairs took place sometimes annually, sometimes many times a year, their dates fixed by the church calendar. Most of them have survived to the present day. To the delight of many August tourists and visitors, a number coincide with the feast of the Assumption of the Blessed Virgin Mary, which is celebrated on 15 August. This is the date of the annual fair at La Bastide-du-Salat in the *département* of the Ariège, as prescribed long ago in its charter of 1346. The bastide of Lagarde in the same *département* holds its annual fair around the same religious feast. Similarly, at Mirande, a bastide founded in the Gers in 1281 by the Comte d'Astarac and the abbot of Berdoues in *paréage* with King Philippe III; its arcaded square and the streets lined with half-timbered houses are still thronged with farmers at the fair held on the Monday after the feast of the Assumption (as well as on Easter Monday and Whit Monday).

Drive some 45 kilometres east from La Bastide-du-Salat along the D117 and you reach La Bastide-de-Sérou, where the annual agricultural fair begins on 5 January, the day before the church celebrates the coming of the three Magi with gifts for the infant Jesus. Whereas the August fair is the only one hosted at La Bastide-du-Salat, the citizens of La Bastide-de-Sérou prospered and still do so by holding lesser fairs on the first Saturday of each month. Mirepoix, one of the finest bastides in the Ariège or indeed in the Languedoc, still hosts fairs not only on the first and third Mondays of every month but also two others, one fifteen days after Easter Day, the other eight days after the feast of Pentecost. Chalabre in the Aude, as well as holding fairs on the second Wednesday in every month, hosts specially important ones on Easter Saturday, on the Saturday before the Ascension, and three days before Christmas. Eymet in the Dordogne holds its fair on 25 November, the feast of Saint Catherine.

At these fairs the farmers and their families brought the produce of the local countryside – around Mirepoix today not only cereals, grapes, garden vegetables and wine but also cattle, pigs and sheep, around La Bastide-du-Salat and La Bastide-de-Sérou orchard fruits, too – to sell in the bastide. Other goods were also bought and sold at such annual events as the craft fair held at Sauveterre-de-Rouergue at Pentecost, and the horse and cattle fairs of Villefranche-du-Périgord, held respectively on 11 November and 4 December. Vergt in the same département has a Tuesday fair occuring twice a month which sells calves.

Many of these fairs lasted upwards of a week, and some still do. Libourne hosts two fairs annually, each lasting eight days, the first around Palm Sunday, the second in November, around the feast of Saint Martin of Tours. The annual threshing festival of the bastide of Le Salvetat-Pyralès in the Aveyron lasts a fortnight, ending on the feast of the Assumption.

These major commercial events which proved vital for the prosperity of bastides were and still are supplemented by the local markets, sometimes held fortnightly, sometimes weekly, in the shade of the market halls or the bastides' churches. At various times in the year the markets would specialize in seasonal offerings, as today the Saturday markets of Villefranche-du-Périgord are devoted to chestnuts and cèpes in September, October and November.

A bastide was designed to bring new lands under cultivation. This explains why so many monasteries and lords were willing to conclude acts *paréage*, relinquishing the site of a bastide in return for an influx of labourers who would till their fields and guarantee their revenues. Often a bastide was founded in a forest, with an eye to eventually clearing it for cultivation. Vergt in the Dordogne lies in what was once the Barade forest, which had a reputation as the haunt of cut-throats and brigands that lasted until the nineteenth century. In the same *départment* lie Molières, which the English founded in 1284 in the midst of the Bessède forest, and Saint-Aulaye, in the Double forest.

Bastides, then, were products paradoxically of war and peace, founded as bastions of fiercely dynastic monarchies yet usually built in the quiet intervals between vicious wars. They were founded for economic reasons, and were also an inspired response to a demographic problem of unusual urgency. No doubt many of the citizens their charters attracted were virtually homeless. Others were on the run, including brigands who had left the armed bands that roamed much of Aquitaine.

These new citizens also included former serfs. The term serf, though derived from the Latin for slave, is not quite the same. Slaves were usually former prisoners of wars against the barbarians. Serfs, by contrast, voluntarily bound themselves to a master in return for a house, a vegetable garden and some land worth clearing and cultivating, though a part of the produce was to be rendered to the master. If the serf ran away, his master had the right to pursue him with any means. In return the master was obliged to protect his serf against any ill.

This was a privileged condition, and in the twelfth century many a free man parted with his liberty for the benefits of serfdom. There were of course disadvantages. Serfs could be sold. A parchment of 1420 in the municipal archives of Saint-Emilion records the sale by Bernard de Caupenne of Saint-Pierre-d'Avesan in the Médoc of his serfs Peyrot de Brenas and Motinet de Villfranca to a merchant of Bordeaux named Richard Manakan. Unless a serf ran away, his or her only way of escape was the church, for by joining even a minor order of the ministry such a person's earlier vows were nullified.

The second major source for peopling a bastide was the French peasant. A peasant's life in the twelfth and thirteenth centuries was hard and exhausting. Again the church, and perhaps the army, was the only way of escape from this condition, until a new chance was offered by the bastides. Even when confined in a bastide, the growing population often burst its bounds. In 1315 the citizens of Marmande in the Lot-et-Garonne made a formal complaint to Edward 11 that the inhabitants of nearby Castelnau-sur-Gupie, a bastide founded in 1276 by Edward 1, were continually invading other people's property.

Such a growth in population obviously alarmed the great seigneurs of Aquitaine and Gascony, giving another impetus for founding bastides along with the political and military ones we have already observed. In fact, documents of this era often refer to these new towns as 'bastidas sive populationes', that is 'bastides or centres of population'. Edward I certainly realized this, founding for example Vergt in the Dordogne in 1285 in *paréage* with Count Archambaud 11 of Périgord with the precise object of gathering within its walls the scattered population of peasants in the surrounding countryside.

The strategy worked. Attracted by the promised rights and privileges, outsiders, disaffected serfs, unhappy peasants, outlawed folk who longed for a return to human society all flocked to the bastides. The new citizens were expected to build their own houses. Inevitably they used whatever local material was available, wattle and daub, stone or brick, though the charter of Bruges in the Pyrénées-Atlantiques specified that the façades must be built of stone. Many bastide houses today are elegantly faced, some three storeys in height, but evidently they were initially much simpler, with a ground floor serving either as a shop, stable or workshop, while the upper storey served as living quarters for the entire family.

By 1329, 610 men, women and children lived in Monflanquin. In 1365 the Black Prince made a census in Périgord with the aim of levying an extra tax on each household. His returns reveal the vast shift of population caused by the building of bastides. He recorded 200 households in Eymet, in Beaumont-du-Périgord and in Vergt, with almost the same number of inhabitants in Villefranche-du-Périgord. Monpazier proved the sixth largest town in his French realms, with 315 households, comprising a population of maybe 1000 souls.

As we have already seen in the reaction of the bishop of Rodez to the foundation of Villefranche-de-Rouergue, which proceeded to steal his subjects, not every great lord warmed to the establishment of a free city near his own domains. In the *département* of Lot-et-Garonne, Xaintrailles has a château (today open to the public) which was rebuilt by Pothon de Xaintrailles, one of the companions of Joan of Arc. Not far away are the bastides of Lavardac and Damazan. To the rage of the lord of Xaintrailles, a good number of his former subjects emigrated there, preferring a life of considerable freedom in one of the bastides to feudal subservience under his protection.

For similar reasons, it sometimes proved no easy task to mark out plots of land outside the bastides for future clearance and cultivation by the inhabitants of these new towns. Outside Monségur local petty lords claimed land which the founders of the bastide wished to use, and twenty-two years elapsed before the dispute could be resolved by appeal to lawyers and the justices of the king of England. Similarly, the monks of La Sauve-Majeure for a long time hampered the development of Créon, claiming land which its citizens eventually were to till. At Sauveterre-de-Guyenne, Edward I was compelled to obtain land from rebellious lords outside his bastide by use of force, only thus managing to fulfil the promise of its charter that 'every citizen of the same town shall retain lands and possessions outside the town, such as two oxen can reasonably cultivate in a year, as well as an acre of land to provide him with grass and what he needs for food.'

Not everyone worked the land. Masons and carpenters; turners, wickerworkers, weavers; men and women who looked after animals and those who dealt in them; leatherworkers who would also skin the animals and cure their hides; candlemakers and smiths; salt-workers, butchers, shopkeepers and taverners are all mentioned in contemporary documents, as well of course as the clergy and lawyers. Bastides needed charcoal burners and barrel makers, cobblers and coppersmiths, glove makers, saddlers and boilermakers.

As well as providing security and an ample livelihood for all these citizens, the bastides were concerned with matters of justice, administered by the bailiffs and the citizens' elected representatives. At Blasimon in the Gironde the contract of *paréage* signed between Abbot Martin of the Benedictine abbey of Blasimon and the seneschal of the king of England offered the seneschal a thousand emplacements beside the local château for building houses. The seneschal agreed to buy from the abbey its woodlands, save for a portion reserved for the monks' own use. They agreed amicably on who should build which fortifications. A town crier was to be employed to make announcements on behalf of the king and abbey alike.

Item six promised that the king and the abbot would build a prison in the bastide. Violence and theft were particularly excoriated, theft including such frauds as watering down wine. To judge by the respective fines levied on consorting with prostitutes and on committing adultery, the latter was considered a much more serious offence, fornicators fined usually ten sous for each night of wickedness, adulterers paying 100 sous and also often publicly humiliated. Different bastides had different standards. At Monflanquin the citizens seem for the most part to have turned a blind eye to debauchery, its ladies of the night inhabiting the carrérot des Cabannes. By contrast, at Puymirol the citizens were particularly harsh, committing adulterers to the pillory and cutting off the hand of crooked lawyers.

As well as being charged with mending roads, collecting levies, repairing bridges and seeing to the defence of a bastide, hygiene and health particularly preoccupied the bailiffs and consuls (sometimes known as *jurats*) who administered these towns. Since there were no public abattoirs, they were insistent that the fetid remains of animals should not lie long in the streets. At Villeneuve-sur-Lot dung and straw thrown into the streets was similarly frowned on, and its citizens were obliged to move it within a week in summer, within a fortnight in winter.

Barber-surgeons, as elsewhere at that time, utilized herbal remedies as well as blood-letting. Leprosy was particularly feared. In the Gironde the bastides of Cadillac, Monségur and Sauveterre-de-Guyenne all set aside little colonies, known as *cagoteries*, for their lepers. The number of beasts they could herd was restricted (at Monségur as we have seen, limited to one pig, twenty sheep and a ram, and six geese). Their animals were strictly prohibited from public ways and from pilgrimage routes.

In spite of such public health measures, the bastides did not escape the Black Death. The disease ravaged Boulougne-sur-Gesse in the Haute-Garonne in 1348. It reached Mirepoix with devastating results in 1361, a mere six years after the bastide had suffered from one of the vicious raids of the Black Prince. (He sacked Plaisance-du-Gers and Saint-Lys in the Haute-Garonne in the same year.) Later in the century the bubonic plague was killing the citizens of Carbonne, south of Toulouse, and Revel, a bastide founded in 1342 fourteen kilometres south of Puymirol. Nor did plagues stop after the fourteenth century. In 1482 the parliament of Toulouse itself fled to the bastide of Saint-Félix-Lauragais to escape one. Nearly everyone died of the plague at Vianne in 1630. Another outbreak cut down the citizens of Monségur as late as 1652.

At such times recourse to prayer was probably as good a remedy as recourse to barber-surgeons. In good times and bad the church played a central role in the life of any bastide — so much so that the act of *paréage* of Blasimon expressly forbade anyone to build a church inside its walls to rival that of the Benedictine monastery. Churches were repositories of precious communal texts and the bastide's seal. Often fortified, they also served as a further defence should the walls of a bastide be breached in time of war. Thus citizens in a bastide lived under the protection of God and their own defences.

In spite of its central importance in the citizens' lives, the church rarely appears at the physical heart of a bastide. Usually off-centre, often at an angle to the market square, where they do not predate the foundation (as at Bla-simon), they also took much longer to build than the rest, in part because to build these mighty churches was a large undertaking.

Religious festivities mingled readily with secular ones, and still do. In particular, the patronal festivals of bastides are so frequently linked to the feast of the Assumption that to list all the relevant ones would be tedious. A good handful are found in the *département* of the Ariège: La Bastide-du-Salat, Lagarde, Montjoie-en-Couerns and Rimont. Montpézat in the Gers holds its patronal festival and communal festival on the same day. In the Dordogne, 15 August is festival day at Villefranche-de-Lonchat and Villefranche-du-Périgord.

To divert themselves on religious occasions was a notable habit of the inhabitants of the bastides. Especially as Lent approached, they enjoyed fairs, and in some bastides used any excuse to introduce a few more into Lent itself. The approach of Palm Sunday and Easter offered another couple of excuses for hosting a fair. So did Christmas Eve. And most of these fairs have survived to this day.

The tradition of celebrating holy days in a secular as well as a religious fashion has persisted, too. The bastide of Cologne celebrates 15 and 16 August with concerts. Also in the *département* of Gers, at the unfinished bastide of Sainte-Radegonde the patronal festival takes place on the nearest Sunday after 15 August, while Montréjeau in the Haute-Garonne has enlivened the religious feast with an international festival of folklore.

Plagues and the Hundred Years War were scarcely over before south-west France and its bastides were embroiled in the wars of religion. Martin Luther was an Augustinian monk, and many of his co-religionists, includ-ing those of Monflanquin, seemed particularly susceptible to the Reformation he preached. A monk named Guillaume Pierre was the first Monflanquin Augustinian to be burnt at the stake in Bordeaux for heresy, having preached the Reformation at Villeneuve-sur-Lot. Not every monk of Monflanquin followed his example in becoming Protestant, and some were still Catholic when their convent was set on fire in 1569 duing the wars of religion.

As we have already seen at Puymirol, warlike Huguenots were particularly keen to burn down churches. Four years before they set fire to the convent at Monflanquin, Protestants had destroyed the church of Notre-Dame-des-Misères at the bastide of Mirabel north of Montauban, in the same year pulling down the church at nearby Réalville. In 1568 they destroyed the abbey of Gaillac-Toulza in the Haute-Garonne as well as wrecking the nearby bastide of Le Plan. The following year their co-religionists in the Landes conquered the bastide of Cachen and burned down its church. In 1572 the church in the bastide of Dourgne in the Tarn was burned down by Huguenots. A year later they pulled down the abbey at Saint-Sever-de-Rustan in the Hautes-Pyrénées. At Domme, hidden behind a Renaissance gateway, you can still find an Augustinian priory founded in 1375 which the Protestant captain Geoffroy de Vivans in part demolished in 1588.

Both Protestants and Catholics sometimes attempted to destroy whole bastides. The Protestants sacked Saint-Sulpice in the Tarn in 1562 and wreaked havoc at La Bastide-du-Salat two years later. They set Barcelonne-du-Gers on fire in 1569 and again in 1591. The following year Cordes-Tolosannes in the Tarn-et-Garonne fell victim to their fervour. In 1578 they sacked Sainte-Foy-de-Peyrolières in the Haute-Garonne.

At other times the Protestants were content merely to capture a bastide from the Catholics and hold on to it, taking for instance Fleurance in 1562 and Villeréal and Villefranche-du-Queyran in 1569 (though a later legend grew that they massacred 1200 Catholics in Fleurance church). The Protestant leader who turned Catholic to become King Henri IV of France made the bastide of Puycasquier in the Gers one of his strongholds. Libourne, a Catholic stronghold in mainly Protestant territory, resisted their assaults, with the result that the bastide was repeatedly attacked.

As for the Catholics, probably their most vicious leader in this part of France during the wars of religion was Blaise de Montluc, run a close second by the Duc de Joyeuse. Montluc was also a brilliant commander.

Born in 1500, he began his military career first as a page and then an archer in the service of the duke of Lorraine. Captured at the battle of Pavia, he was released and distinguished himself at the battle of Siena in 1555. King Charles IX, who under the influence of his mother Catherine de' Medici had authorized the infamous massacre of Protestants on Saint Bartholomew's Day, 1572, made him seneschal of Guyenne, where he was ruthless in the pursuit of Huguenots.

Montluc conquered and savagely punished the citizens of Villefranche-de-Rouergue for espousing the Reformation. He did the same at Sauveterre de Guyenne. He also took and savaged Labastide-d'Armagnac in the Landes. In 1562, Blaise de Montluc had all the Protestants of Lectoure killed and thrown into a well as their common grave, observing that this was a 'very fine dispatch of extremely wicked persons'. Then he partly pillaged the town. In the same year his men took on and routed a Protestant force of 500 just ouside Vianne. After the battle some 300 were buried in Vianne, though many others drowned trying to swim across the River Baïse. Eight years later the bastide of Rabastens-de-Bigorre, 19 kilometres north-east of Tabes, was in his hands. At this siege, however, he was wounded and disfigured by a shot from an arquebus. In consequence he gave up his command and retired to write his memoirs, which the future Henri IV described as 'the soldier's breviary'. In them Montluc noted with regret that at the battle of Vianne he had too few troops to kill all the enemy, adding, 'As for taking prisoners, one never spoke of that in those days.'

The viscount of Panat, an old enemy of the Duc de Joyeuse and lord of Réquista in the Aveyron, had embraced Protestantism. In 1586 his bastide was pillaged by Catholic troops commanded by the duke. Four years later Joyeuse was in the Haute-Garonne, taking back from the Protestants the bastide of Montastruc-la-Conseillière, which he proceeded to ravage.

When Louis XIII came to the French throne after the assassination of his father Henri IV in 1610, he confirmed the Edict of Nantes, which from 1598 had secured a large measure of religious liberty to French Protestants. None the less he and particularly his minister Cardinal Richelieu (who virtually ruled France from 1629) set about destroying the defences of former Huguenot strongholds. Inevitably, bastides were among them.

Their zeal in putting down Huguenots became all the stronger after the Protestants rose up again when Catholic rights were restored in the Béarn in the early seventeenth century. Though it took time for Richelieu to reassert his authority throughout the land, their revolt was put down by 1622, and their former strongholds further weakened. Mauvezin, in the *département* of the Gers, had so enthusiastically embraced Protestantism that it was dubbbed 'little Geneva'. Richelieu had its defences stripped down in 1621. During the same war the Protestant stronghold of Lavardac was taken and ravaged by the Catholic Duc de Mayenne. Most of the ramparts of Laparade, a bastide founded by Alphonse de Poitiers in 1269 some 25 kilometres west of Villeneuve-sur-Lot, were dismantled as soon as the revolt had been put down. So were those at Puymirol. The ramparts of Revel, which had changed hands too often for the cardinal's liking during the conflict, were demolished in 1629, as four years later were those of Réalmont south west of Albi. At Sainte-Foy-la-Grande the Protestants had strengthened its fortifications in 1585 by building a citadel. It was demolished in 1635.

The fate of Monflanquin offers a delicious historical irony. Richelieu ordered that the stone of the ramparts, which he had demolished in 1632, should be used to rebuild the Augustinian convent which the Protestants had partly ruined. Meanwhile the Protestants installed themselves in part of the church of Notre Dame, before building their own church in place Caladon. They were expelled from it and their church in its turn destroyed when Louis XIV revoked the Edict of Nantes in 1685. Unlike many Huguenots who fled the country, some of the Protestants of Monflanquin struggled on, until by an imperial decree of 1805, Napoleon Bonaparte gave them the former Augustinian chapel.

Yet the destruction wrought in that era was great. Bastides, though by no means impregnable, posed a threat to the monarchy unless their defences were weakened. So again, on the orders of Louis XIII the bastide of

Rocquefixade in the Ariège lost its château in 1632, after an abortive revolt of the governor of the Languedoc.

Fascinatingly, in 1631 when Cardinal Richelieu was building his own château beside the River Mable much further north in the *département* of Indre-et-Loire, he commissioned the architect of the Sorbonne, Jacques Lemercier, and his brother Pierre to build next to it a defensive town to house his court. It was designed precisely like a bastide, rectangular, measuring some 500 by 700 metres, and surrounded by walls and gates. Long, straight streets cross each other at right angles. In the place du Marché is a market hall with fine carpentry. Offset from the market square is the parish church. The Grand'Rue even has a seneschal's house. Jean de La Fontaine described this town as 'the most beautiful village in the universe'. But though it looks like a bastide, and was obviously modelled on them by the cardinal who had been obliged to behave so destructively to some of them, it is not one. The citizens had no charter; and Richelieu also commissioned the Lemerciers to build him a great ducal château in the nearby park, which dominated his town until it was pulled down in 1805.

The two greatest Protestant strongholds in the realm were the port of La Rochelle south west of Poitiers and the altogether remarkable bastide of Montauban in the Tarn-et-Garonne. From 1627, Richelieu's troops besieged La Rochelle for fifteen months; when the starving inhabitants finally surrendered their numbers had fallen from 28,000 to 5000.

Already in 1621 he had besieged Montauban with 20,000 soldiers. The bastide was defended by 4500 persons, led by the Protestant Pastor Chamier and the Consul Dupy. After investing Montauban for three months, Richelieu withdrew the siege. The success of the defendants was a tribute not only to their own courage but also to the strength of the fortifications which the Huguenot Duplessis-Mornay had built around the city in 1585.

The history of the bastide is much older than this. In the ninth century Archbishop Théodard of Narbonne founded an abbey at a spot called

Montauriol which rises beside the River Tarn and on the Roman road from Toulouse to Cahors. The abbey flourished, attracting around it a village to whose inhabitants Alphonse Jourdain, count of Toulouse gave a charter in 1144, offering them free citizenship of a fortified town which they should build on a plateau named Montauban, rising not far away over the river. Most of the people of Montauriol happily escaped the taxes and servitude of their former state into the new town, as did numerous serfs. The new foundation rapidly prospered, its later privileges including the right of self-government by ten elected consuls (who here, like those of Toulouse itself, were known as *capitouls*). Regular markets, pilgrims, visiting merchants, the river traffic and the town's windmills increased its wealth.

Chequerboard streets lead to the heart of Montauban, its great, arcaded market square (today the place Nationale). Set at an angle to this impressive regularity, its parish church, dedicated to Saint James the Great, was begun in the thirteenth century and, apart from its vaulting and furniture, finished in the fifteenth, with the addition of a Gothic, machicolated Toulouse-style belfry, whose three octagonal storeys, built of rose coloured brick, rise above the river.

Though Montauban was fortified, Simon de Montfort took it during the Albigensian crusade, but Count Raymond VI of Toulouse took it back in 1220. After the treaty of Meaux, the bastide's first fortifications were demolished. With the deaths of Alphonse de Poitiers and his wife in 1271, the bastide became part of the kingdom of France. In 1304, Philippe IV gave Montauban authority to build a bridge across the Tarn. Finished in 1335, its tall pointed arches have stood for six centuries. Montauban became a bishopric in 1317, and at the treaty of Brétigny of 1361 was ceded to the English, at which the Black Prince enlarged the fortress which protected the bridge and made Montauban an English stronghold face to face with Toulouse.

Outside the bastide's walls, though still under its protection, were founded convents and also the episcopal city, for here civil and ecclesiastical powers were kept separate. Finally Protestantism triumphed at Montauban in 1561. One of its bishops, Jean de Lettes de Montpezat, was among those who embraced the new faith – though perhaps for the wrong reasons. At his consecration in 1539 he had engraved on the episcopal ring Virgil's line, 'Love conquers everything, and we give way to love.' In Jean de Lettes's case, the beloved was a woman named Armande de Durfort, and for her he abandoned his bishopric and the abbey of Moissac, embraced Calvinism and with his bride retired to Geneva, where he died in 1559.

Jean fared better than other members of his family. His nephew Melchior de Montpezat remained a Catholic, remarking insouciantly during the troubles, 'I remain at ease, employing most of the time dressing my dogs and birds.' The Huguenots poisoned him. His brother, Bishop Jacques des Prés was more aggressive, not to say warlike. He took to putting on his armour and hunting down Protestants, who lured him into an ambush in 1589 and killed him.

At Montauban churches and convents were closed down, and on 20 December 1561 the Protestants forced the doors of the cathedral of Saint Théodard, pillaged the interior and set it on fire. They spared the church of Saint James the Great which was now devoted to the Protestant cult. Henri of Navarre, the future Henri IV of France, founded a Calvinist college in the bastide and Marguérite of Navarre founded an academy for training Protestant pastors.

Then occurred one of two events which make Montauban so unusual a bastide. In 1614 a fire destroyed the western and southern arcades of the place Nationale. The architect Pierre de Levesville restored them, with a double arcade. The second event was another fire, this one destroying the arcades on the northern and eastern sides of the place Nationale. This time the architect responsible for rebuilding was Bernard Campmartin. The result is an arcaded market square, built of warm, narrow bricks, which apart from the ogival arches of the covered walks displays with relish the seventeenth-century neo-classical style. At the apex of each round arch is a boss. Square pilasters rise above them, flanking three storeys which increase the illusion of height by being less tall as they rise.

One further monument here testifies to the religious controversies of the seventeenth century. After the revocation of the Edict of Nantes, the Catholics decided to build a new cathedral in Montauban. To find space for it, the architects (François d'Orbay and his brother in law Robert de Cotte) had to destroy a whole sector of the original layout of Montauban. Its foundation stone was laid in 1692, and the cathedral of Notre-Dame was completed in 1739. This is a deliberately singular building, in a classical style reminiscent of the churches of the Jesuits and standing out from the rest of the brick-built bastide by being faced in stone.

The citizens for the most part remained resolutely Protestant. Economically the next century was a golden age, as it was architecturally. Growing rich on the silk and wool trade, the bourgeoisie built themselves elegant town houses, with balconies and inner courtyards. With the exception of its cathedral, Montauban remains a superb urban ensemble.

Until the Revolution the only challenge to the French monarchy after these religious disturbances, was the Fronde, a series of civil wars during the minority of Louis XIV between 1648 and 1653 when the princes and the Paris parlement sought to curb the royal powers. Although they caused disturbances in the provinces, they scarcely seem to have affected the bastides, though Miradoux in the Gers was besieged by Prince Louis de Condé, who had turned against his cousin the king, and Caudecoste in the Lot-et-Garonne was taken by him in 1651. He also arrived at Fleurance in the same year, a town reduced to some misery during the wars of religion, a condition rendered worse by the fact that it had been forced to garrison the royal troops. Before Condé could do much damage, a yet worse disaster occurred in an outbreak of the bubonic plague.

Happily, the fortunes of Fleurance picked up during the next century, and the bastide began to flourish again on agriculture and commerce, developing new industries until the outbreak of the Revolution. The Revolution itself was kinder to some bastides than to others. At Montpezat in 1793 the seigneurial château was dismantled and the collegiate church transformed into a temple of reason and half demolished. Monpazier, which had been a Protestant stronghold at the time of Geoffroy de Vivans, took the opportunity of vilifying its religious orders, and the order of Recollects was expelled from the bastide. The citizens had little cause to thank the *ancien régime*, having endured over a century of poverty: more than a hundred of its citizens died of hunger in 1693. Still, it seems unjust for their descendants to turn on the Recollects, for during the eighteenth century they and the confraternity of White Penitents had cared for countless poor. Fortunately the citizens were wise enough not to destroy the Recollects' convent, which was put to secular use as a meeting place for the whole community. Vianne, by contrast, elected eleven citizens as its revolutionary committee and, in conformity with the law of 22 March 1794, they proceeded to sell by auction the furnishings of their church (and that of nearby Calezun) to replenish the public purse.

Domme cannily played its part in the Revolution without sacrificing any of its own interests. One of its citizens of that era, Jacques de Maleville, is today honoured with a bust on the esplanade overlooking the Dordogne. He had risen from obscurity ('mediocrity' was his word) as he put it 'by my own efforts and parsimony, reaching where I am today in spite of having had to bring up six children at home'. No friend of the monarchy or what he described as the old, corrupt church, Jacques de Maleville represented Domme in the councils of the Revolution. He was one of the editors of the new civil code. A gifted pamphleteer, he published one in 1801 defending the separation of quarrelsome married couples and even divorce as better than 'scandal, shouting matches, family quarrels and the hatred which can only set a bad example to children'.

Other children of bastides were yet more distinguished in these heady times. In 1767, Joachim Murat was born at Labastide-Fortanière in the Lot, rising from humble beginnings to become one of Napoleon's generals, the emperor's brother-in-law, and king of Naples. In 1836 his birthplace changed its name to Labastide-Murat in his honour.

The intellectual ferment of the nineteenth and early twentieth centuries did not entirely pass the bastides by. No doubt most families carried on their traditional ways, sometimes impoverished, sometimes not. Domme, meanwhile, bred another revolutionary, Paul Leclus, a friend of the Russian anarchist Prince Peter Kropotkin. Leclus is honoured today by a museum of local history, at one side of Domme's market square, a museum far more devoted to old ploughs, ancient costumes and local history in general than to the man after whom it is named. Tourism and antiquity has overwhelmed political passion.

Tourists should not, however, be derided, for in this part of France some of them have brought a sympathy and concern that has helped to transform many a declining and consequently dilapidated bastide. A remarkable example is offered by the first bastide of all. By the end of World War 1 Cordes was in a deep decline. Its golden age had lasted until the mid-fourteenth century, with a hundred weavers working under the protection of the bastide. The wealth they engendered helped to create such exquisite buildings as the houses of the Grand Fauconnier, the Grand Veneur and the Grand Ecuyer. Cordes still prospered in the next century, adding a nave to its parish church. But the plague and the religious wars plunged the bastide into misery. Many citizens abandoned the spot. From around 1730 the bastide recovered a little, with the introduction of mechanical looms, but by the early twentieth century few of these were still in use.

Revival began with the discovery of the bastide by the painter Yves Brayer in 1940. Brayer dubbed Cordes 'the Toledo of the Tarn'. He bought a house there and gathered around him friends and other artists, who set themselves up as an academy of art and began restoring the tumbledown houses. Although Yves Brayer was increasingly occupied in Paris, where he was responsible for the new decor of the Opéra, he continually returned to the bastide. His inspiration was carried on by a local vigneron and artist named Jean-Marc, who set up his workshop in Cordes in 1958, dividing his time between sculpture and caring for his vineyards. Other artists, sculptors, jewellers, craftsmen and craftswomen followed. Today Cordes blossoms, traffic-free, immaculately preserved, with workshops and booths, stalls and shops offering visitors the work of the artists who have colonized and restored to new life France's very first bastide.

Gazetteer

No attempt is made to list all the surviving bastides, but the reader should find mentioned here those which remain superb or have a particular interest. Entries are arranged alphabetically by *département*, to make it easier for the traveller to locate those bastides nearest to his or her route; market days, fairs and festivals are given at the end of each entry.

An asterisk directs the reader to the index, from which fuller information on the place, person or topic indicated may be traced through the body of the book.

Ariège

CAMARADE, a fortified village 10 kilometres west of the celebrated caves of Le Mas-d'Azil (which were occupied in 30,000 BC), was a bastide built on the site where prehistoric families also made their homes, their chief legacy the dolmen of Commenge. It prospered on salt mines, but fell into decline after Louis XIII ordered the demolition of its château in 1625 at the end of the second phase of the wars of religion. The former bastide has retained its much restored fortified church; vines, cereals, sheep, pigs and beef cattle are raised in the surrounding fields; while visitors and locals hunt and fish.
Patronal festival: 24 June (birthday of Saint John the Baptist).

CAMPAGNE-SUR-ARIZE was founded in 1255 by the Comte de Foix in *paréage* with the abbey of Bonnefont. Set amid vines and orchards in the Arize valley north-west of Foix, this vestigial bastide nowadays prospers on cattle, sheep and cereals. Campagne-sur-Arize helped to transform the River Arize into a defensive frontier, aided by the bastide of Montesquieu-Volvestre 10 kilometres north-west in the *département* of the Haute-Garonne and La Bastide-de-Besplas, which lies beside the river half-way there, as well as by La Bastide-de-Sérou further south (see below).
Patronal festival: 22 July (feast of Saint Mary Magdalen).

❈ LA BASTIDE-DE-BESPLAS was founded by the Comte de Foix in 1255. Set in the valley of the Arize, amid vineyards and orchards as well as fields full of cattle and sheep, its chief attraction is the ruined château de Baillard. The bastide grew up around a chapel, known as the Bout-du-Pont, which lay at one end of a bridge across the river and was founded by the lord of Baillard who built the first château here. Its successor is the eighteenth-century chapel of Notre-Dame-du-Bout-du-Pont. Today a new château has been built in the town park. The parish church dates from the nineteenth century, with modern stations of the cross by Léon Zak.

Fairs: second Tuesday of each month.

Patronal festival: 29 September (feast of Saint Michael the Archangel).

❈ LA BASTIDE-DE-BOUSIGNAC, once a dependency of the lords of Mirepoix, is today a village in the Coutirous valley at the eastern end of the *département*. Its church still preserves a medieval gable-belfry, and near the village stand the ruins of a medieval chapel of Notre-Dame.

Patronal festival: 30 November (feast ot St. Andrew).

❈ LA BASTIDE-DE-LORDAT was called La Bastide-de-Gerderenoux until the Revolution. Set in the Hers valley, which is enlivened with the colours of tobacco and cereals, its nineteenth-century church shelters an eighteenth century marble high altar with a gilded tabernacle and a statue of the Virgin Mary. Some of the craftsmen are skilled ironworkers.

Patronal festival: 3 August (a feast which in medieval times commemorated the legendary discovery in the year 415 of the bones of Saint Stephen, the first Christian martyr).

❈ LA BASTIDE-DU-SALAT was once a small fortress, founded in the twelfth century, which gathered around it citizens who were given a charter of customs as a bastide in 1346. Two hundred years later, during the wars of religion, Protestants devastated the bastide, which was restored with strengthened defences in 1610. This little bastide, now given over to holidaymakers, lies beside the poplar-shaded River Salat, amid fields where sheep and cows graze and vines, cereals and tobacco grow. Sporting facilities include fishing and hunting. The bastide boasts a windmill and an eighteenth-century church which guards a sixteenth-century Pietà in painted wood.

Patronal festival: first Sunday after 15 August (feast of the Assumption).

LA BASTIDE-DE-SEROU was founded in 1252 after an act of *paréage* between the Comte de Foix and the abbey of Combelongue. It stands in the Arize valley (see Campagne-sur-Arize and La Bastide-de-Besplas, above and Montesquieu-Volvestre in in the Haute-Garonne). Prehistoric people inhabited the region, as did the Romans. The prehistoric legacy can be explored in the underground caves of Garosse and Quérénas (the former with wall paintings). Although La Bastide-de-Sérou suffered during the wars of religion, which saw its Catholics put to the sword, it retains some of its fortifications and a fine market square. Here too is its ruined fortress, and the fourteenth-century keep of a château which belonged to the Foix family. Dating from the sixteenth and seventeenth centuries, the parish church houses several earlier statues, including a late fifteenth-century gilded Pietà, a fifteenth-century statue of Jesus and a sixteenth-century painted relief of the Deposition. Visitors are offered camping facilities.
Fairs: first Saturday of each month.
Patronal festival: 24 June (birthday of Saint John the Baptist).

LAGARDE, set on a plateau overlooking the River Hers, was once part of the lordship of Mirepoix which Simon de Montfort gave to Guy de Lévis. The château which the Lévis family built here was demolished at the time of the Revolution, but situated in a park remains a superb ruin, dating from the fourteenth to the sixteenth centuries, incorporating the remains of a Renaissance chapel, with stables, a still discernible double ring of fortifications and a defensive ditch. The church of the former bastide dates from the nineteenth century. The town prospers on woollens as well as farming.
Festival: around 15 August (feast of the Assumption).

MAZERES was founded in 1253 by an accord between the Comte de Foix and the Cistercian abbey of Boulbonne. The present abbey of Boulbonne is not the original, which rose on a site 12 kilometres upstream of the Hers. This was one of the most impressive of the region, indeed of the Midi. Here on 12 September 1213, just before the battle of Muret, Simon de Montfort* consecrated his sword to God and the Blessed Virgin Mary. During the wars of religion the Protestants destroyed the abbey.

Gaston *Fébus was born here, and in 1390 welcomed the king of France with a vast herd of cows, their horns painted blue, which was the chief colour of his coat of arms. The rectangular plan of a bastide remains, but the château of the Comtes de Foix is no more, burned down in the early sixteenth century. At the heart of the bastide is a huge market hall, with intricate carpentry. Here too is a Gothic church, the medieval house of the Comtes de Foix, a sixteenth-century presbytery with a Renaissance staircase tower, and an eighteenth-century bridge across the river.

Another celebrated warrior who inherited this bastide was Gaston de Foix, born at Mazères in 1489. Nephew of King Louis XII of France, he became duke of Nemours, fighting brilliantly in the Italian wars, defeating the Swiss, the troops of the papacy and the Venetians. His troops also defeated the Spaniards at Ravenna on 11 April 1512, but Gaston himself perished in this battle. His lands were transferred to the kingdom of Navarre, and when Henri de Navarre became king of France the country of Foix was finally joined to the possessions of the French crown.

Fairs: agricultural concourse at the beginning of April, festival of force-fed geese and ducks at the end of December.

Patronal festival: last Sunday in July.

Festival of flowers: Ascension week, when around twenty decorated floats parade the streets.

MIREPOIX is superb, strategically huddled between the Pyrenees and the Garonne plain. The Gauls and the Romans lived here, and the town is first recorded in written history in 1062. In 1207, Comte Raymond-Roger de Foix gave its citizens a charter of rights and privileges. The town had already become a stronghold of *Catharism, with some 600 believers and several 'perfects' living within its walls. Accordingly Simon de Montfort, hammer of the heretics, successfully laid siege to Mirepoix in 1209 and gave the town to his lieutenant Guy de Lévis, who was created marshal of Mirepoix, charged with controlling the whole region.

Disaster struck in 1279, when the town was flooded and virtually destroyed. Its consuls urged Guy III de Lévis to rebuild on a safer site and he chose the confluence of the Rivers Hers and Countirou. The work was carried out by his son Jean, who built a classic bastide, with two major lateral streets forming the basis of other streets laid out in chequerboard fashion and converging on a central arcaded market square surrounded by covered walkways.

Although Mirepoix was devastated by the Black Prince in 1355, ravaged by the plague in 1361 and set on fire by bandits in 1363, its pattern, restored in the fourteenth and fifteenth centuries, remains classic. Wooden pillars support the half-timbered houses of its market square. As at *Monpazier, the corners of this square form deliciously arched angles. On the joists of the maison des Consuls are carved entertainingly grotesque heads, some human, some depicting monsters.

Mirepoix became a bishopric in 1317, its bishop another member of the Lévis family. Bishop Philippe de Lévis was generous to his home town. In 1298 his forebears, Jean I de Lévis and his wife Constance de Foix, had founded here a sandstone church dedicated to Saint Maurice (commanding officer of the Theban Legion, 6600 men who were martyred in the reign of the Roman emperor Maximian for refusing to make heathen sacrifices). From 1327 it was transformed into a fitting cathedral, the work completed only in the fifteenth century. Its octagonal belfry, with a crocketed spire, rises to 60 metres. A late fifteenth-century Gothic doorway gives access to a huge nave, 48 metres long, 22 metres wide and 24 metres high. Such a massive space proved difficult to vault, and the present ceiling, with its sculpted bosses, dates only from 1867. Five chapels radiate from its polygonal apse. Nearby is Philippe's episcopal palace.

The bastide was once fortified, though only the fourteenth-century *porte d'Aval* still stands, grooved for its portcullis and inscribed with the town's former coat of arms. In time of war, the citizens could drink from the Cordeliers' fountain.

Mirepoix today has adapted itself to tourism, with camp sites and sporting facilities, including horseback riding.

Fairs: first and third Mondays of each month; 17 January, 30 July, 21 November.
Patronal festival: 22 September (feast of Saint Maurice and the Theban Legion).

◪ MONTARDIT in the valley of the Volp was once a bastide whose defensive aspects are today revealed only in its own fortifications and its fortified church.
Patronal festival: 9 September.

◪ MONTJOIE-EN-COUSERANS derives its name from a temple to Jupiter (*Mons Jovis*) which once stood on this defensive site. Here, in *paréage* with the bishop of Couserans, Alphonse de Poitiers founded a bastide around 1256. What remains is the bastide's rectangular fortifications, a fourteenth-century defensive wall 48 by 45 metres, pierced by two gateways. They guard sixteenth-century half-timbered houses and at the centre of the bastide a massive fourteenth-century church, whose fortified façade has two battlemented galleries and a couple of octagonal towers. Nearby the spa of Audignac-des-Bains still attracts visitors.
Festival: 15 August (feast of the Assumption).

◪ RIMONT, in the valley of the Baup 35 or so kilometres west of Foix, lies on the site of the Premonstratensian abbey of Combelongue, founded here around 1175. In 1272 the monks, in *paréage* with Eustache de Beaumarchais, seneschal of the king of France, founded a bastide which commanded the route to the River Sérou. On 21 August, 1944, retreating Nazis set fire to the bastide and almost completely destroyed it. Rebuilt, it retains some remnants of its former ramparts and part of a twelfth-century church which once served as the abbey's chapel.

Fairs: first and third Mondays of each month; 15 days after Easter Day; 8 days after Whit Sunday.
Patronal and communal festival: 15 August (feast of the Assumption).

ROQUEFIXADE rises on an exceptionally fine site, surveying the rocher de Monségur and the massifs of the Saint-Barthélemy and the Trois-Seigneurs. A château was built here in the eleventh century and after the defeat of the Albigensians came into the possession of the kings of France. Philippe le Hardi bought it in 1270, and transformed the village into a bastide, giving it a charter of customs in 1288. Rebuilt from the thirteenth to the sixteenth centuries, today the château is an evocative ruin.
Patronal festival: 16 June.
Communal festival: first Sunday in July.

VILLENEUVE-DU-LATOU, a dependency of the château of Latou lying in the valley of the river of that name, was called Villeneuve only after receiving its charter as a bastide in the thirteenth century. Older than the bastide, its eleventh-century parish church has a delicious polygonal apse.
Patronal festival: fourth Sunday in September.

VILLENEUVE-DU-PAREAGE, derives its name from the bastide set up in 1308 by an act of *paréage* between King Philippe le Bel of France and the bishop of Pamiers. The church dates from the nineteenth century.
Patronal festival: 22 November.

Aude

*CARCASSONNE, a jewel among the fortified cities of France, divides itself into two. The upper city, restored by France's greatest nineteenth century Gothic architect, Viollet-le-Duc, and his pupils, is a dream city, with 3 kilometres of ramparts bristling with 35 defensive towers. This is not the bastide of Carcassonne, which constitutes the lower city and is fully described (in chapter 1). The city is much devoted to the needs of tourists, with horse riding, hunting and other sports readily available.
Market: Tuesday, Thursday, Saturday.
Fairs: 6 March, first Saturday of September, 25 November.

CHALABRE, set where the rivers Hers, Blau and Chalabreil meet, was transformed into a bastide at the end of the thirteeenth century by the lord of Bruyères. Its château, greatly restored from the fifteenth to the nineteenth centuries, stands in an extensive park. The church of Saint Peter dates from 1552.
Market: Saturday.
Fairs: second Wednesday of each month; Easter Saturday; Saturday before Ascension Day; 3 days before Christmas.
Patronal festival: four days around Ascension Day.

LABASTIDE-D'ANJOU, in the Fresquel valley, is as its name implies a former bastide founded by Louis d'Anjou, seneschal of the king of France in 1370. Its fifteenth- and sixteenth-century houses often have dates over their lintels. The church dates from the nineteenth century (a seventeenth-century one now transformed into a hall).
Festival: 29 August.

LA DIGNE-D'AVAL is one of the comparatively rare circular bastides. Built beside the River Cougain near Limoux, the external wall of its double ring embraces two gateways, while the internal one is pierced only by one.
Festival: 27 July.

MOLANDIER, which today reveals scarcely a sign of its former bastide pattern, was founded in 1246 by the Comte de Foix in *paréage* with the lord of Belpech.
Festival; 15 August (feast of the Assumption).

RIBOUISSE was founded in 1270 or 1271 by Guy de Lévis on a plateau above the Vixiège and still preserves a house bearing his coat of arms, as well as a fourteenth-century Languedoc Gothic church. Look out for the thirteenth-century statue of Saint Christopher in the wall.
Festival: 19 and 20 August.

SAINT-DENIS, situated on a flank of the Montagne-Noire, was founded at the end of the thirteenth century by Philippe Le Bel. Its charters gave the citizens the right to hunt in the Serre forest, and its consuls continued to govern the bastide until the Revolution. The Romans inhabited the site. Of the bastide remains the rectangular rampart and walls, with a gateway of 1616. The church of

Saint Denis (traditionally the first bishop of Paris, who missionized the Gauls in the mid-third century) is fourteenth-century Gothic in style, with ogival chapels and a fifteenth-century Madonna.
Fair: 1 August.
Patronal festival: around 9 October (feast of Saint Denis).
Summer festival: end of July – beginning of August.

Aveyron

LA BASTIDE-L'EVEQUE was founded by Bishop Raymond de Calmont of Rodez in a fit of pique at the foundation of *Villefranche-de-Rouergue in his domains. In spite of its splendid site, close by the gorges of the Aveyron, it never rivalled Villefranche-de-Rouergue. But it remains charming, with a church built in the fourteenth and fifteenth centuries that boasts a gable-belfry at its west end.
Communal festival: first Sunday in August.
Patronal festival: 18 November.

LA SALVETAT-PEYRALES is a bastide founded in the thir-teenth century which grew out of a *sauveté. Long administered by jurats, today its ancient legacy includes the ruined château of Peyralès, its keep and curtain wall set on a peak, and the fifteenth-century ruined château of Roumégous, whose huge square keep has circular angle towers. The church is nineteenth century; the banks of the rivers slope into vineyards and fields with cereals and cattle.
Fair: 6th of each month.
Patronal festival: first Sunday in September.
Threshing festival: 1 August to 15 August (feast of the Assumption).

⚔ NAJAC, was founded by Count Alphonse de Poitiers. Simon de Montfort had occupied the site, though it seemed impregnable, during the Albigensian crusade, and in subsequent centuries the bastide repeatedly changed hands between the English and the French. Slate-roofed houses (including one once occupied by the seneschal), some of them with wrought-iron balconies, are guarded by the remains of its fortifications, and the communal fountain dates from the fourteenth-century. A rose window, a thirteenth-century processional cross, a fifteenth-century hexagonal tower, fourteenth- and fifteenth-century statues and sixteenth-century stained glass windows are some of the delights of its parish church. The bastide offers tourists fishing, canoing and cycling.
Patronal festival: Sunday after 24 August.

⚔ REQUISTA, a bastide founded in 1293 by the count of Rouergue, was set on fire by the English in the fourteenth century and sacked by the Catholic troops of the *Duc de Joyeuse in 1586. Its château is today a picturesque ruin, its church nineteenth century Gothic. Lying in the valley of the Tarn, Réquista has retrieved some of its former importance by attracting visitors to its markets, fairs, and festivals.
Market: Sunday.
Fairs: Second Thursday of each month; 20 November (horse fair).
Patronal festival: Sunday after 28 August.
Sports festival: second Sunday in July.

⚔ *SAUVETERRE-DE-ROUERGUE is fully described else-where in this book save for the information that the English occupied it twice during the Hundred Years War and for information about its festivals.
Fairs: Whitsun (crafts), last Sunday of October (chestnuts and sweet cider).
Melon festival: first Sunday in September.
Patronal festival: last Sunday in July (Saint Christopher).

⚔ VILLECOMTAL, in the valley of the Dourdou with its chestnut-clad hills, is a bastide founded at the end of the thirteenth century by the count of Rouergue, who gave it its charter of customs. Surrounded by the remains of its former fortifications and its two defensive gateways, the streets criss-cross at right angles. Châteaux and their keeps add more defences to Villecomtal and its four-teenth-century three-aisled Gothic church.
Fairs: monthly.
Patronal festival: 24 August (feast of Saint Bartholomew).

VILLEFRANCHE-DE-PANAT obtained its charter of franchises from Count Pierre de Panat on 15 September, 1297. Set beside a 5 kilometre-long lake, the bastide has become a centre of tourism, while still trading the local beef cattle and sheep.

Market: Friday in summer (stalls tend to close down in the afternoon).

Fair: fourth Sunday of each month (livestock).

Festival: 14 July (Bastille Day), celebrated with fireworks, brilliantly reflected in the lake.

 *VILLEFRANCHE-DE-ROUERGUE is exhaustively described in Chapter 2.

Market: Thursday.

Fairs: 22nd of each month.

Patronal festival: 6 June.

 *VILLENEUVE, 10 kilometres north of Villefranche-de-Rouergue, was recreated as a bastide around 1269 by Alphonse de Poitiers. Earlier Bishop Pierre 1 Bérenger of Rodez had founded a *sauveté* here, on a plateau close by a Benedictine priory. The church of the bastide, dedicated to the Holy Saviour and initially modelled on the Holy Sepulchre in Jerusalem, is in origin Romanesque. The nave and polygonal choir date from the fourteenth century, as does the Romanesque octagonal tower. The frescoes of the apse are exceptionally fine, thirteenth-century in date. A gilded and painted statue of the Virgin and Child, dating from the sixteenth century, blesses the choir.

Villeneuve's market square is still arcaded and the two town gates are impressive, protecting what today is an unpretentious, charming town.

Market: Saturday.

Fairs: first day of each month.

Dordogne

*BEAUMONT-DU-PERIGORD, set on a hilly site near the River Couze, was founded by the English seneschal Lucas de Thenay in 1272.
Fairs: second Tuesday of each month.
Festival: 15 August (feast of the Assumption).

BEAUREGARD-ET-BASSAC is a bastide set on a hill above the valley of the Crempse which was founded by the English in 1268. Its market hall dates from the twelfth century; its Gothic church has been greatly restored and has a modern belfry, whereas in neighbouring Bassac the church is Romanesque. The sixteenth-century château de Beauregard still stands. The countryside around Beauregard-et-Bassac is devoted to growing strawberries and tobacco.
Festival: 15 August (feast of the Assumption).

*DOMME, though crammed with visitors in summer, is one of the most entrancing bastides in France, an acropolis above the fertile valley of the River Dordogne, where grow walnuts, maize, tobacco, vines and poplars, where truffles abound and geese are force fed to produce foie-gras.
Market: Thursday morning.
Folklore festival: first Sunday in June; second fortnight of July.

*EYMET, founded by Alphonse de Poitiers in 1256, received its charter of rights and privileges four years later. The church of Saint-Sulpice derives (with many restorations) from the chapel of the Benedictine priory which predated this bastide. Eymet's prehistory is well set out in the local museum, which is housed in part of what remains of its fourteenth-century fortress.
Market: Thursday.
Fair: 25 November (feast of Saint Catherine of Alexandria).
Patronal festival: last Sunday in July.

Dominating the Alzou gorge, Rocamadour has remained a premier French pilgrimage site since the Middle Ages.

A treasured resident rests after keeping clean the streets of Molières.

The bastide of Cazals was founded in 1319 by Guillaume de Toulouse on behalf of the King of England. Little seems to have changed since then.

At Carbonne the sleepy church overlooks the river.

Is this citizen of Fleurance, the capital of the land of Gaure in Gascony, meditating on the town's long history or wondering whether to take a drink in a local bar?

At Montcléra a crowned statue of the Virgin Mary blesses the town, herself blessed by a winged cherub.

The fourteenth-century octagonal tower of the cathedral at Rieux-Volvestre rivals those of the celebrated brick-built churches of Toulouse itself.

The château of Bonaguil, with its thirteen towers, is set in woodlands and represented the chief feudal threat to the neighbouring free citizens of such bastides as Montcabrier and Villefranche-du-Périgord.

At Sauveterre-de-Rouergue look out for little bas-reliefs: a woman and baby on the wall opposite the grocer's shop, and this one of three gloomy faces contemplating a hare.

Throughout the region of the bastides, charming remains from the Middle Ages reveal themselves, this one at Saint-Antoine-la-Vallèe.

*As in many French towns in bastide country, the church
at Montesquieu is the predominant feature, save for the
exquisite surrounding countryside.*

The houses of Revel, a bastide founded in 1342 by King Philippe VI de Valois, display a beguiling mixture of brick and stone.

Set peacefully beside the river and an ancient bridge, the church of Rieux is a powerful defensive building, capable of withstanding assaults, as well as a house of God.

Our forefathers' genius for creating delightful patterns out of simple materials is no better displayed than at Plaisance-du-Gers.

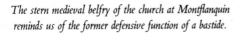

The stern medieval belfry of the church at Montflanquin
reminds us of the former defensive function of a bastide.

A quiet corner of the Romanesque monastery of
Moissac.

Every fortified town needed its well, such as this one at
La Bastide-l'Evêque.

(OVERLEAF) *As this double gateway reveals, the*
citizens of Beaumont, a bastide founded in 1272, had no
intention of welcoming invaders.

Saint-Lizier boasts a cathedral, a cloister and an
episcopal palace, but its charms also reside in half-
timbered houses such as this.

Half-timbered houses at Aïnhoa in the Pyrénées-
Atlantiques.

FONROQUE, a bastide founded by Edward I in 1284, still retains vestiges of its defensive walls, while the modern parish church incorporates a fifteenth-century doorway.
Patronal festival: feast of the Holy Trinity.

*LALINDE, founded in 1267 by the English seneschal Jean de Lalinde on behalf of King Henry III, though ravaged by retreating Nazis in 1944, remains delightful, not least for its site beside the River Dordogne, the Bergerac wine of its taverns, and the varied layout of its fields, devoted to orchards, maize and tobacco.
Fairs: second Thursday of each month.
Festival: Sunday after 29 June.

MOLIERES is one of those bastides which never came successfully to fruition. Founded by the English in 1284 in the Bessède forest and near the River Belingou, it ought to have had every chance of succeeding, based on a site inhab-ited since prehistoric times and beside a thirteenth-century château (now in ruins). Molières none-the-less has some sweet houses and a thirteenth-century church with a square belfry, Gothic doorways, and a Romanesque font.
Fairs: first Friday of each month.
Festival: Sunday after 24 June.

*MONPAZIER, by any account a prime bastide, beautifully pre-served, features extensively in the rest of this book.
Every week its superb arcaded central square is filled with a colourful market.
Market: Thursday.

SAINT-AULAYE, a bastide founded in 1288, rises high above the River Dronne and formerly guarded the entry into Périgord from the Charente. Its town hall is an impressive, much restored twelfth-century château and its Roman-esque church is beautifully decorated.
Market: Saturday.
Fairs: fourth Tuesday of each month; 10 September.
Patronal festival: second Sunday in May.

*VERGT, founded by the English in 1290, scarcely resembles a bastide today, save that its citizens seem to have inherited some of the entrepreneurial skills of their enterprising ancestors and since 1950 have made the town the strawberry capital of France. In 1562 a vicious, inconclusive battle took place outside Vergt between Catholics and Protestants.

Market: Friday.

Fairs: second Tuesday of each month (calves); first Friday of January, Good Friday, 26 June.

*VILLEFRANCHE-DE-LONCHAT, founded by the English seneschal Jean de Grailly in the 1280s on a site once inhabited by Gauls and Romans and where a church (the église de Lopchac) had stood since the eleventh century, still boasts – outside the town – a huge three-aisled Gothic church with a fourteenth-century crypt, a twelfth-century font and a pentagonal, ogival-vaulted apse. From the bastide a panorama extends across the Lidoure valley and to the western limits of the *département* of the Dordogne.

Market: first and third Thursdays of each month.

Festival: 15 August (feast of the Assumption).

*VILLEFRANCHE-DU-PERIGORD was called Villefranche-de-Belvès, taking its name from the nearby Augustinian monastery of Belvès when Alphonse de Poitiers founded the bastide in 1261. Its development into one of the finest bastides in the Dordogne (its major features described elsewhere in this book) was much encouraged by Edward 11 of England, to whom it passed in 1287.

Market: Saturday.

Fairs: 11 November (horses), 4 December (cattle).

Festival: 15 August (feast of the Assumption).

Gard

*AIGUES-MORTES is the only bastide in the Gard, a coastal fortress created by Saint Louis, that is to say King Louis 1x of France. It is an oddity among the bastides, far more forbidding than any other. At the same time, as Henry James put it, if Aigues-Mortes is dead, 'it is very neatly embalmed.' In its early years the bastide housed around 10,000 people (and still houses 4500). After the revocation of the Edict of Nantes, which had brought a temporary measure of toleration to Protestants, the Catholics imprisoned Huguenot women in the *tour de*

Constance, one unfortunate soul named Marie Durand kept here for 37 years until her death. Earlier the tower had served as a prison for the unjustly disgraced Knights Templars. These unhappy prisoners inscribed graffiti on the walls (as the Templars also did when they were imprisoned in the *porte des Tours* at the bastide of *Domme in the Dordogne).

Louis 1x earned his canonization for his zeal in crusading against Muslims. In place Saint-Louis at the centre of Aigues-Mortes is a statue of the pious persecutor, sculpted in 1849. Nearby is a seventeenth-century Capuchin convent, now an exhibition centre. In rue Gambetta rises a hospital founded in 1347. The church of Notre-Dame-des-Sabliers was begun in the thirteenth century, from which era derives its central aisle, the rest of the building added in the eighteenth century.

From the fourteenth century the port of Aigues-Mortes began to silt up, and the bastide gradually fell into decline. Even so, the decline was only a comparative affair. Religious orders continued to establish themselves here, the Grey and Blue Penitents in the seventeenth century, both orders building chapels which still survive, as does the seventeenth-century convent of the Capuchins. In terms of its architecture, whatever its eventual decline, Aigues-Mortes blossomed again in the seventeenth century.

Market: Wednesday, Sunday.

Patronal festival: first Sunday in October (includes bull-running).

Festival: August; medieval re-enactments including knights on horseback.

Gers

BARCELONNE-DU-GERS was created in 1316 by an agreement between King Philippe v le Long of France and the prior of Saint Gilles, representing the order of Saint John of Jerusalem (Knights Hospitallers). Initially known as La Bastide de Gosset, the bastide took the more grandiose name Barcelonne only in 1343. Strategically sited above the meandering River Adour and amid the regions of the Béarn, the Chalosse, the Bigorre and the Armagnac, Barcelonne-du-Gers was bound to become a prized site in times of war; indeed, it suffered greatly during the fourteenth-century struggles between the Armagnacs and the counts of Foix and in the religious conflicts of the sixteenth century, so much so that parts of the town were several times set on fire – twice by the Protestants, in 1569 and 1591.

Yet its wide central square and its straight streets still evince a typical bastide, as does the church of Notre-Dame, rebuilt in the sixteenth century but retaining its single nave, its ogival choir and its mighty square belfry. Nothing remains of the former fortifications.

Fairs: monthly except September (two in October).

Patronal festival: 14 July (also Bastille Day).

Communal festival: Palm Sunday.

BARRAN, stretching alongside the River Baïse, was created after an act *paréage* signed in 1278 by the count of Armagnac-Fezensac and the archbishop of Auch. (A village already existed here, a staging post on one of the pilgrimage routes to Santiago de Compostela.) A year later the new citizens were accorded their charter of customs, and soon the new town was inundated with families. A list of them, drawn up in 1303, still survives. So do some remnants of the town walls, a delighful bridge across the moat and a square town gate, 7 metres wide and 10 metres high. Barran has also preserved an arcaded central square and some chequerboard patterned streets. The sixteenth-century parish church of Saint John the Baptist is also a treat. It boasts a thirteenth-century spire, made of wood and covered in slates which ingeniously twist.

Barran is a centre for rearing spirited race horses, as well as fowl, beef cattle, pigs and sheep. Vines and cereals also thrive outside its walls.

Fair: 1 August.

Festival: last Sunday in August.

BASSOUES, set upon a ridge over the valley of the Guiroue, instantly reveals itself as a bastide by its ruler-straight streets, its central square and the deft carpentry of its sixteenth-century market hall. The square is shaded by half-timbered houses and is the site of the bastide's well. Nearby is the fourteenth-century church of Notre-Dame, with its square belfry, and a font, a stone pulpit and a Pietà all dating from the fifteeenth century.

The archbishop of Auch founded this bastide in 1278 close by the site of a Benedictine convent, and the citizens received their charter in 1295. In places you can make out the original fortifications. Unusually in a bastide, around 1365 a château (restored in the sixteenth and seventeenth centuries) with a magnificent keep was built here, on behalf of Archbishop Arnaud Aubert, who was the nephew of Pope Innocent VI. The four storeys of the keep rise to 43 metres, carrying 4 bartizans, while each wall is 8 metres wide and supported by powerful buttresses. It houses an interesting museum of local history, concentrating on the *castelnaux, sauvetés* and bastides of Gascony.

Fair: 17 January.

Patronal festival: feast of the Holy Trinity.

BEAUMARCHES, like many bastides, is named after its founder, in this case Eustache de Beaumarchais, seneschal of Philippe le Bel, who concluded an act of *paréage* with the count of Pardiac in 1288. Although the bastide did not flourish, its Gothic church, built from the fourteenth to the sixteenth centuries, has a monumental porch which matches that of Villefranche-de-Rouergue and is decorated with a frieze of entertaining faces.

Patronal festival: 8 September.

BRETAGNE-D'ARMAGNAC lies some 25 kilometres south-west of Condom beside the River Izaute and the three lakes known as Zou-Fou-Dou: it is thus a perfect centre for water sports. In the thirteenth century the bastide was known as Villa Comitalis, and was a major stop for pilgrims journeying to Santiago de Compostela, who would stay at the hospice of Saint Jacques which once stood at the eastern entrance to the town. It is possible that the name Bretagne-d'Armagnac derives from Bretons, making that pilgrimage, who decided to make their homes here. Rebuilt as a bastide in the thirteenth century, the town possesses a regular central square, and a church with a Romanesque porch.

Communal festival: third Sunday in July.

*COLOGNE, on the banks of the Serrampion, is described in detail elsewhere in this book. This bastide has a particular charm because its houses are so diverse, some of brick, others of cob, others of stone, others of wood. Inside its church is a sixteenth-century gilded Pietà, sculpted out of wood, as well as an altarpiece of the style favoured by the architects of Louis XIV. The treasury is well worth a visit, its liturgical gems mostly dating from the seventeenth and eighteenth centuries. Cologne presents musical evenings on 15 and 16 August.

Patronal festival: around 15 August (feast of the Assumption).

*FLEURANCE, founded by Eustache de Beaumarchais in *paréage* with Géraud de Cazauban, count of Gaure and lord of Saint-Puy, was ruled according to its charter of 1278 by four consuls. The bastide became English in 1279 and remained so until the fourteenth century. Although Fleurance is triangular in shape, the various parcels of land on which the citizens built their houses are square, each 60 metres by 60 metres. The bronze fountains at each corner of the monumental, nineteenth-century market hall are by A. Durenne and represent the four seasons. Most of the arcaded houses surrounding this square date from the eighteenth century. The town hall dates from 1834–7.

East of the bastide alongside the River Gers, Fleurance has developed a leisure centre, and the town has also promoted horse racing, fishing and camping.
Market: second and fourth Tuesdays of each month.
Fairs: first and third Tuesdays of each month.

FOURCES, a rare circular bastide though its streets still run chequerboard fashion, is defended to its south-east by a massive fifteenth-century château and by the *tour d'Horloge*, which was once a defensive gate in its former fortifications. Plane trees shade its central square, which is surrounded by half-timbered houses jutting out over arcaded walks. Edward 1 gave the bastide its charter of rights and duties in 1289. The medieval church at Fourcès has preserved its square, aggressive belfry. The bastide hosts six fairs a year.
Communal festival: first Sunday after 15 August (feast of the Assumption).

GIMONT, initially called Francheville, is a bastide founded in 1265 by the abbot of Planselve and Alphonse de Poitiers and lying on the left bank of the River Gimont. Its right-angled streets and its wooden market hall are charming, some of the houses flanking them half-timbered. In shape this bastide is long and narrow, some 1000 metres by 300 metres. The church was built in stone and brick from the fourteenth to the fifteenth centuries. A single nave, reaching a choir with radiating chapels, shelters two sixteenth-century crucifixions, both carved out of wood.
Market: first Wednesday of each month.
Fairs: first Wednesday in Lent (geese and ducks); last Sunday in April (ham).

JEGUN, the Celtic etymology of whose name (meaning vine) indicates the antiquity of the site, is built on a spur overlooking the Loustère. A fortified *castelnau* existed here in the 1170s, and the bastide is based on this foundation. Perfectly regular, it lacks a central square, and the market hall (topped by a neoclassical building) simply tucks itself amongst the half-timbered and stone fifteenth- and sixteenth-century houses. Jegun also lacks a church, relying on the Romanesque pilgrimage church of Sainte-Candide outside the new town.
Markets: second and last Thursdays of each month.

Fairs: second and last Thursdays of October, November, December.
Patronal festival: 4 December.
Communal festival: first Sunday in September.

⊠ LANNEPAX (which means land of peace) is a thirteenth-century bastide which has preserved remains of its fortifications, once pierced by four gates. A rectangle 280 by 160 metres, the bastide is divided into twelve blocks, one of which constitutes the market square. At one corner of the square rises the church of Saint Jacques (this bastide being on a route to Santiago de Compostela), built in the thirteenth century, its north side added in the next, its belfry free-standing. Three parallel streets, some of them with half-timbered houses, run east–west, bisected by three others running north–south. A document of 1290 reveals that a lawyer was already living here by then, but there is no certainty about who founded this bastide – though we know that the counts of Armagnac levied taxes here.
Goose fair: first Sunday after 1 November (All Saints' Day).
Patronal festival: last Sunday in July.

⊠ MARCIAC, situated at the confluence of the Laus and the Arros, took its name from Philippe le Bel's seneschal Guichard de Marciac, who founded the bastide in 1298 in *paréage* with the abbot of la Case-Dieu and Arnaud Guilhem III de Monlezun who was count of Pardiac, each of them agreeing to take a third of the revenues of their new foundation. In that same year citizens were enticed to the bastide by the proclamation of a charter of rights and privileges. So as not to offend the local lords of Villecomtal, Tillac and Monlezun, it was agreed that no citizen should be welcomed from their territories for six years.

Once again this is an exquisitely regular bastide, each extremity turning itself into an oval. The arcaded market square, whose hall disappeared in the nineteenth century, is vast, 130 metres by 75. A splendid fourteenth-century parish church, with a square belfry that becomes octagonal and was topped by a spire in the nineteenth century, welcomed pilgrims on their way to Santiago de Compostela. So in medieval times did four hospices, now all gone (save for the Augustinians' fourteenth-century belfry). At 90 metres, the belfry of the parish church is the highest in the Gers. Inside the church, its three aisles and pentagonal apse house fourteenth-century sculptures.
Market: Wednesday.
Fairs: first Wednesday in each month; Wednesday following 8 September.
Patronal festival: last Sunday in August.

MASSEUBE, with its right-angled streets, regular blocks of houses and arcaded central market square, began life as a Gallo-Roman site. Its name means 'farm in the forest', and by the thirteenth century it consisted of a farm in thick and extensive woodlands belonging to the Cistercian abbey of the Escaladieu. In 1274 the abbot and Count Bernard IV of Astarac in *paréage* founded the bastide, issuing its charter two years later. The market hall and the church sit virtually side by side, the latter's three aisles replacing the original monastery church, the hall carrying the former communal meeting place which is now the mairie.

Now devoted in part to tourism, Masseube has not lost its traditional pattern of life.

Market: 1 August (livestock).

Fairs: Easter Monday, last Sunday in May and July; third Sunday in September (grape harvest).

Patronal festival: Sunday following 25 July (feast of Saint James of Compostela).

*MAUVEZIN, whose medieval charters date from 1230 and 1276, is blessed with a magnificent fourteenth-century market hall surrounded by arcaded houses. The post office dates from the sixteenth century and is known as the house of Henri IV. Follow rue du Vieux-Temple and you reach the square tower named after Henri IV's mother, Jeanne d'Albret. The bastide's church, dedicated to Saint Michael, has an octagonal stone belfry built in the thirteenth century. (The rest of the church was rebuilt in 1829, though it shelters fifteenth-century choir stalls which came from the bastide of Barran.)

Mauvezin is a bastide of narrow streets, some of them steep. It is celebrated for its garlic.

Market: Monday.

Pig fair: second Monday in the month.

Other fairs: Easter Monday: Monday following the last Sunday in September; first Monday in November.

MEILHAN was a bastide, receiving its charter from the Comte d'Astarac and the abbot of Berdoues in 1280, but it has lost all traces of the original foundation. Today its chief attraction is the thirteenth-century ruined château and — a more melancholy monument — a stele just outside the village under which lie the mortal remains of 84 members of the French Resistance, killed in a battle against the Nazis on 7 July, 1944.

Patronal festival: Sunday nearest 29 June (feast of Saint Peter and Saint Paul).

Communal festival: second Sunday in October.

*MIELAN, created in 1284 by Eustache de Beaumarchais and Guill-aume de la Roche and named after the Italian city of Milan, though set on fire by the English in 1370, rebuilt and occupied again in 1450, still has its arcaded market square, fourteenth-century houses with corbelled balconies (especially in the rue de la Ritourie), and a windmill. Its church dates from the nineteenth century. The lake of Miélan has allowed it to develop as a centre for water sports. The farmers breed horses as well as cattle.

Market: second Thursday of each month.

Fairs: first Thursday in February; Thursday before 25 August.

Communal festival: last week in August.

MIRADOUX, founded in 1253, is the oldest bastide in the Gers. Its fortified parish church, which dates from the thirteenth century, has a sixteenth-century porch, three aisles and a polygonal apse, as well as ogival vaulting. The belfry was never finished. The market hall rises on stone pillars.

Festival: around 25 August.

MIRANDE is a well preserved bastide 25 kilometres south-west of Auch, on a route which shortly afterwards reaches the bastides of Miélan (above) and Rabastens-de-Bigorre (Hautes-Pyrénées). Founded in 1281 by an act of *paréage* between the king of France, the Cistercian abbey of Berdoues and the Comte d'Astarac (the remains of whose château, built in the twelfth century by Comte Bernard IV d'Astarac, can still be seen). Mirande was founded on 5 May 1281, the same day as Pavie (see below) and by the same founders.

Its orthodox bastide pattern developed around two axes, each 430 metres long, flanked by seven blocks of houses each 52 metres square. Although the market hall was demolished in the nineteenth century (to be replaced by a band-stand), its central square is arcaded. Vestiges of ramparts still protect fine houses dating from the fifteenth to the eighteenth centuries, some with half-timbered façades. The Gothic church of Notre-Dame is equally outstanding, especially its buttressed belfry which was fortified in the fifteenth century, and its sculpted doorway. Inside are fifteenth-century stalls and magnificent sixteenth-century stained glass, said to be by the glazier of Auch cathedral, Arnaud de Moles. At the edge of the town is an eighteenth-century hospice which once sheltered pil-grims to Santiago de Compostela.

Market: Monday.

Fairs: first and third Mondays of each month; Whit Monday, Easter Monday, Monday after the feast of the Assumption and the feast of Saint Denis (9 October), a religious pattern which indicates their antiquity.

Patronal festival: 15 August (feast of the Assumption).

🏴 *MONTFORT-DU-GERS, which received its charter and franchises from Comte Géraud v d'Armagnac in 1275, boasts a central arcaded square with a market hall topped by what was once the communal meeting hall. At one side stands the thirteenth- and fourteenth-century church, with a single nave and to the north side an octagonal tower rising from a powerful stone base. The restored fifteenth- and sixteenth-century château d'Esclignac, with its two vast courtyards and its drawbridge sits impressively in its park. Montfort's windmill no longer works.

Patronal festival: Sunday following 15 August (feast of the Assumption).

Communal festival: last Sunday in May.

🏴 MONGUILHEM, created in 1319 by Annet de Toulouse in *paréage* with Guilhem de Montaigut, seneschal of the Marsan for King Edward 11 of England, retains its central square and a fortified fifteenth-century church, built of brick. Its charter, issued in 1320, required the citizens to appoint a town crier as well as a lawyer. This is a countryside of polyculture and (being close to the *département* of the Landes) of Armagnac liqueur.

Patronal festival: 10 June.

🏴 MONTPEZAT is a small, unusually irregular bastide, founded in the late thirteenth century and still retaining its former market hall. The church was rebuilt in 1840.

Patronal festival: 15 August (feast of the Assumption).

🏴 MONTREAL-DU-GERS, the second oldest bastide in the *département* (see Miradoux, above, for the oldest) was founded on 30 March 1255 by Alphonse de Poitiers and Baron Géraud de Fourcés, who charged a lawyer from Agen named Pons Maynard to mark out the plan of the new town, fixing the positions of its squares, tracing the future streets and the blocks of houses, and finding a site for the church. He was also commissioned to edit the charter of customs, and to nominate six consuls. The charter decreed that the French king, represented by his bailiff, was the sole lord of Montréal-du-Gers, that market day should be Tuesday and that the citizens were entitled to hold two annual fairs. The bastide was completed by 1289.

Defended by rectangular fortifications and a square gateway, from east to west Montréal-du-Gers is cut by five parallel streets, three of them the main thoroughfares. Three other streets cross them at right angles, dividing the new town into rectangular blocks. The houses are half-timbered and encorbelled. A vast market square, with stone arcades, and a Gothic church, partly fortified, its doorway monumental, are characteristic marks of a late thirteenth-century bastide. The town rises on a defensive escarpment on the right bank of the River Auloe. Yet the site and the fortifications did not make the bastide impregnable. It borders on the Landes, 15 kilometres to the west, where the English mostly held sway, and is only five-and-a-half kilometres from the English bastide of Fourcès. From its foundation, and especially during the Hundred Years War, Montréal-du-Gers repeatedly passed from the French to the English and back again. Today its vineyards flourish and the prized local drink is Armagnac.

Fair: Monday before Christmas.

✠   PAVIE, founded on 5 May 1281, (the same day as its sister bastide Mirande, above) by Comte Bernard IV d'Astarac in *paréage* with Philippe le Bel and the Cistercian abbey of Berdoues, has an unusually irregular enclosure, walled in trapezoid fashion, defended by three fortified gateways and six watchtowers (as it needed to be, lying a mere 5 kilometres south of the English stronghold of Auch). A thirteenth century, three-arched stone bridge crosses the River Gers here, and Pavie was obviously created in part to dominate its confluence with the Sousson and the Cédon. Many of its old houses are half-timbered (see especially rue d'Etigny and rue de la Guérite), and the thirteenth-century church of Saint Peter has a fourteenth century belfry. It also shelters a thirteenth-century statue of the Virgin Mary known as Our Lady of the Cédon, which belongs to the chapel of Notre-Dame-du-Cédon (restored in the nineteenth century) to the south of the bastide, and is the subject of an annual pilgrimage on 25 March.

Pavie hosts an international festival of folk dancing at the end of June.

Patronal festival: three days around the last Sunday in June.

✠   PLAISANCE-DU-GERS was founded in 1322 by an act of *paréage* between Comte Jean I d'Armagnac and the abbot of la Case-Dieu. Set out chequerboard fashion and administered by consuls, Plaisance-du-Gers found it difficult to attract citizens, in part because of the nearness of other bastides, in part because of the plague. Another set-back was a vicious act of demolition by the Black Prince in 1355. The bastide has two arcaded squares (see Saint-Clar, below), flanked by eighteenth- and nineteenth-century houses, as well as some earlier half-timbered dwellings. Its inns serve Gascony wine from the côtes de Saint-Mont.

Fairs: first Thursday of each month; Thursday before Palm Sunday; 14 July (goat's cheese fair).

Festival: 14 July (Bastille Day).

✠   *PUYCASQUIER, a bastide created in the thirteenth century by the counts of Fezensagut, has remnants of its thirteenth- and fourteenth-century ramparts, a sixteenth-century market hall, and a church, dedicated to Saint Abdon, whose belfry rises from an ancient watchtower, its upper part octagonal in the Toulouse style. Inside is a thirteenth-century lead font.

Patronal festival: nearest weekend to 30 July; features floats with flowers and folk dancing.

SAINT-CLAR is a Benedictine foundation, set on the banks of the Aratts and the Auroue and created in 1289 by Bishop Géraud de Monlezun of Lectoure (who was feudal lord of the region and had a château here, 15 kilometres from his cathedral), and King Edward I of England. The bastide was preceded by a *castelnau. Its streets criss cross at right angles, and like Plaisance-du-Gers the bastide has two arcaded squares. Its market hall dates from the thirteenth century. Sixteenth-century half-timbered houses still survive here and its windmills have been restored. The parish church was built in the nineteenth century. Fortunately the Romanesque church of the *castelnau* still stands, dating from the twelfth century.

Garlic market: Thursdays; the second largest in France.

Communal festivals: first Sunday in June, third Sunday in September.

SEISSAN began life in the twelfth century as a *castelnau* of the abbey of Faget. Unable to protect its inhabitants, in 1266 the abbot decided to transform it into a bastide, in *paréage* with the Comte d'Astarac. Seissan received its charter of customs in 1288, but scarcely transformed itself into a recognizable bastide. Remains of the thirteenth-century château can still be seen here, and the church is modern. The lake offers scope for water sports.

Market: Friday; November to February, specializes in foie gras.

Patronal festival: first Sunday in September.

Communal festivals: second Sunday in May, 15 August.

SOLOMNIAC on the River Gimone was begun in 1323, the result of an act of *paréage* between the abbey of Gimont and Bertrand de Solomniac, seneschal of Toulouse. In its market square, bordered by fine fifteenth- and sixteenth-century arcades, rises a fourteenth-century market hall, supported by stone pillars. The Huguenots grievously damaged its single-aisled parish church in 1580, and the present building is a seventeenth- and eighteenth-century restoration.

Market: second and fourth Thursdays in each month.

Patronal festival: 9 September.

Communal festival: feast of the Ascension.

VALENCE-SUR-BAISE is the result of an act of *paréage* signed in 1274 by Count Géraud v d'Armagnac and the abbot of the Cistercian abbey of Flaran. The magnificent abbey still stands here, with its twelfth-century Romanesque church (which boasts a rose window and capitals carved with foliage) and the sacristy, the chapter house and cloister. It also houses a museum devoted to the pilgrimage to *Santiago de Compostela.

At Valence-sur-Baïse the place de l'Hôtel-de-Ville is arcaded, and some of the former fortifications still stand. On the north side of the square rises the fourteenth-century parish church, which was well restored in the nineteenth century. Set on a 55-metre hill overlooking the rivers Baïse and Auloue, the bastide was well protected with its walls and four defensive gateways. None the less it passed several times from the French to the English and back during the Hundred Years War.

Patronal festival: third Sunday in June.

 VILLEFRANCHE grew around the château de Castillon, a fortress built in the eleventh century on the right bank of the Gimone. In 1291 the lord of Castillon founded the bastide of Castillon, which soon took on the name Villefranche. The founder confirmed the charter of the citizens in 1297. Yet Villefranche has remained a little bastide, its cob-built houses set alongside two parallel streets and a wide market place. The thirteenth-century church (restored in the eighteenth century) gives on to this square.

Fair and communal festival: Palm Sunday.

Patronal festival: Sunday following 15 August (feast of the Assumption).

Gironde

 *BLASIMON, whose architectural treasures are fully described elsewhere in this book, is in the wine-growing region of Entre-Deux-Mers.

Communal festival: 29 August.

✉ *CADILLAC, mostly described elsewhere, has a superb château built in the sixteenth century by the first duke of Epernon, Jean-Louis Nogaret de la Valette, which suffered depredations in the nineteenth century and was used for a time as a women's prison. Restoration work began in 1852. The château boasts monumental chimneys, and one wing serves as a *maison du vin*. Cadillac's hospice of Sainte-Marguérite was founded in 1617 by the same duke as a shelter for pilgrims. The bastide also has two fine gates, the *porte de la Mer* and the *porte de l'Horloge*.
Market: Saturday morning.
Fairs: 5 January (the eve of the visitation of the Magi); nearest Sunday to 24 August.

✉ *CREON, already described in this book, is the capital of the western region of Entre-Deux-Mers.
Market: Wednesday.
Fairs: last Wednesday of each month, 30 November, Christmas Eve.
Festival: first weekend in September.

✉ *LIBOURNE remained an English bastide until the English quitted France in 1453. In a chapel of the parish church is preserved a spine from the crown of thorns.
Market: Tuesday, Friday, Sunday.
Fairs: from Thursday before Palm Sunday, from Sunday before 12 November (feast of Saint Martin); both last eight days.

✉ MONSEGUR lost its old market hall in 1880, when it was replaced by a cast-iron one. Bordeaux wine is sold in the market.
Market: Friday.
Fairs: 2 January, 24 March.
Patronal festival: nearest Sunday to 25 August (the feast of Saint Louis of France).

✉ PELLEGRUE, a late thirteenth-century bastide founded by the Pelle-grue family, preserves vestiges of its fortifications and the thirteenth-century Romanesque church of Saint Andrew, built like a Byzantine basilica in cruci-form fashion with a dome.
Market: Wednesday.
Fair: second Wednesday of the month.
Communal festival: second Sunday after Corpus Christi.

✉ *SAINTE-FOY-LA-GRANDE, though founded by Alphonse de Poitiers in 1255 on land belonging to a ninth-century Benedictine priory, soon changed hands and remained an English bastide until 1453. It also became Protestant in the sixteenth century.

Market: Saturday (for Bordeaux wines).

Fairs: 20 March, 20 November, New Year's Eve.

Communal festival: around 14 July (Bastille Day).

 *SAUVETERRE-DE-GUYENNE, a fortified bastide created in 1281 by Edward 1 of England and still retaining four gateways from its old ramparts, is a classic bastide. The Knights Templars built a commandery here, and at the nearby hamlet of Le Puch their church, with its sculpted Roman-esque porch, can still be seen. When the bastide took the part of the Reformation, it was viciously punished by troops commanded by Blaise de *Montluc. Culinary delights of Sauveterre-de-Guyenne include lamprey, snails and cèpes.

Fairs: 25 January (feast of Saint Paul), 6 December (feast of Saint Nicholas).

Wine festival: 3 days over last weekend of July.

Communal festivals: 14 July (Bastille Day), 15 August (feast of the Assumption).

Haute-Garonne

ALAN, which was founded in 1270 and received its charter two years later, is blessed with a Gothic gateway set amid the remnants of its medieval fortifications and beside its defensive ditch. The market hall stands on the south side of the central square, while on the east side rises the thirteenth-century church, which boasts a fourteenth-century façade with a gable-belfry and a sculpted frieze.

Alan was a favourite winter retreat of the bishops of Commingues, and their episcopal palace, which dates from the twelfth to the fourteenth centuries, is still here.

Festival: 8 September.

BEAUCHALOT, with its ruined château and church with a defensive tower, is not specially remarkable as a bastide save for its oval shape. Founded in 1327, it received a charter of customs two years later which Philippe de Valois confirmed in 1332.
Festival: Sunday after 1 August.

*BOULOGNE-SUR-GESSE was founded by Eustache de Beaumarchais in paréage with the Cistercian abbey of Nizors. Begun in 1283, the bastide, received its charter three years later. Its finest feature is the Gothic church, with its early sixteenth-century wall paintings and furnishings. Boulogne-sur-Gesse was afflicted by the Black Death in 1348.
Fairs: second and fourth Wednesdays of each month.
Patronal festival: 15 August (feast of the Assumption).

BOUSSENS, a bastide which was jointly founded by the abbot of Bonnefort and the count of Commingues in 1269, still has a Gothic church (with a fourteenth-century gable-belfry and a twelfth-century font). Its artificial lake makes it a venue for water sports.
Festival: 15 August (feast of the Assumption).

CALMONT, founded in the thirteenth century, lost out when its baron became Protestant. The Catholics of Pamiers murdered him, and when the citizens joined the Protestant uprising in the early seventeenth century, the marshal of Thémines burned their bastide to the ground.
Festival: Sunday after 29 November.

CARBONNE, set on the left bank of the Garonne, was founded in 1264. Two years later a bridge spanned the river. Its charter of customs, issued in 1257, was confirmed in 1357. In the meantime the Black Prince had savaged the bastide and later many of its citizens succumbed to the plague. Of the ancient bastide the market hall, and the fourteenth-century church remain.
Market: Thursday.
Fair: second Thursday in the month.
Festival: Sunday after 10 August.

ESPERCE was once a bastide, with a thirteenth-century charter of customs, but it lost all traces of its former self – save for the restored fourteenth-century Gothic church – when the Protestants ravaged the town in 1569.

GAILLAC-TOULZA, founded by Alphonse de Poitiers and

the abbot of the twelfth-century abbey of Calers, was devastated by both sides during the wars of religion. Little remains of the abbey, but the thirteenth-century brick church still stands, with its Romanesque doorway.
Festival: Sunday after 8 August.

G R E N A D E, a bastide founded in 1290 by Philippe le Bel and the monks of Grandselves, retains all the classical features of a bastide, as well as fourteenth- and fifteenth-century half-timbered houses. The eighteenth-century market hall rises from 36 octagonal brick pillars. Commanding the confluence of the Garonne and the Save, Grenade overlooks rich countryside which nourishes cattle and grows fruit in abundance, to be bought at its market and fairs. This is a centre of fishing and horse-racing.
Market: Saturday.
Fairs: second Saturday in March; 18 october.
Patronal festival: 15 August (feast of the Assumption).

*LABASTIDE-CLERMONT boasts the ruined Cistercian abbey of Notre-Dame-de-la-Clarté-Dieu, and a medieval church, the sole surviving monuments of a bastide founded around 1300 by the king of France and the monks.
Festival: third Sunday in September.

L E G U E V I N, though no traces of the bastide remain, is historically interesting as a bastide, founded in 1309, which developed from a commandery of the Knights *Hospitallers.

*MONTASTRUC-LA-CONSEILLIERE, a Hospitallers' foundation transformed into a bastide by Sicard d'Alaman in 1242, became subject to the French throne in 1271. The Protestants took the town in 1570, in response to which it was successfully besieged and devastated ten years later by Catholic troops led by the the Duc de Joyeuse.
Market: Saturday.
Fairs: second Wednesday of each month.
Festival: Sunday after 24 August.

*MONTESQUIEU-VOLVESTRE has a parish church (crammed with masterpieces of religious art, including three fifteenth-century statues of Jesus) dedicated to Saint Victor, whose feast day falls on 21 July – not, oddly, the patronal festival.
Market: Tuesday.

Fair: third Tuesday of each month.
Patronal festival: last Sunday in August.

✠ MONTGEARD, a rose-brick bastide nicknamed for that reason 'little Albi', has a fortified parish church, begun in the fourteenth century and given in 1561 a square machicolated tower. Lierne vaulting inside shelters four alabaster statues in the Renaissance style, depicting the Assumption, the corona-tion of the Virgin, the mystic throne and Saint Catherine. Montgéard became a bastide in 1319, and its partly restored château was finished in 1561.
Festival: Sunday after 15 August (feast of the Assumption).

✠ MONTREJEAU, a foundation of 1272 by Philippe le Hardi in *paréage* with the lords of Espagne-Montespan, means 'royal hill' and the esplanade of its public gardens (with an orientation table) gives extensive views of the surround-ing countryside, with its pastures and cornfields. The central square is arcaded. The church of Saint John the Baptist dates from earlier than the bastide, founded probably in the twelfth century, though its present Gothic form is chiefly fourteenth-century. The octagonal belfry was added in the seventeenth and eighteenth centuries. Inside are some fragmentary wall paintings. An artificial lake has been created beside the Garonne to cater for water sports.
Market: Monday.
Fairs: Monday after 4 March, Trinity Sunday, 24 August and 30 November.
Patronal festival: 24 June (feast of Saint John the Baptist).
International folklore festival: 15 August (feast of the Assumption).

✠ PALAMINY, a fortified thirteenth-century bastide, still boasts two squares and a fourteenth-century church with an impressive gable-belfry.
Festival: 19 June.

✠ REVEL's central place Philippe VI de Valois is beautiful, with covered, arcaded galleries set in houses ranging from the fourteenth to the eighteenth cen-turies and centring on a huge wooden market hall with fourteenth-century car-pentry, topped by a stone belfry (rebuilt in the nineteenth century after a fire). Many of the streets have encorbelled houses, some stone, some brick. The church dates from the nineteenth century.
    The bastide was founded by Philippe VI in 1342. Its charter set out in detail the dimensions of the whole new town. Shortly afterwards, in 1348, Revel was devastated by the Black Death, it suffered the ravages of the Hundred Years War and the wars of religion, and its ramparts were demolished in 1629 on the orders of Louis XIII.

Market: Saturday.
Fairs: first Saturday in February, May, June, September, November.
Communal festival; first Sunday in July.

⚔ *SAINT‑FELIX‑LAURAGAIS existed long before Eus‑
tache de Beaumarchais founded the bastide in the thirteenth century, and the spot
was even inhabited in prehistoric times. A fourteenth‑century château and the
remains of ramparts (including a round tower) protect the bastide, which centres
on its market square and its fourteenth‑century market hall, topped by a belfry and
another hall. The collegiate church dates from the fourteenth century.

Saint‑Félix‑Lauragais was the birthplace in 1167 of Guillaume de Nogaret,
who became chancellor to Philippe le Bel, insulted the pope, persecuted the Jews
of Toulouse and organized the arrest and trial of Jacques de Molar, head of the
Knights *Templars. He died in 1313, a year after he had persuaded the pope to
condemn the whole order.
Market: Tuesdays.
Fairs: Thursday after Whitsun; Tuesday after 1 November (All Saints' Day).

⚔ SAINT‑LYS is a bastide, founded in 1280 by Philippe le Hardi and
given a charter of customs two years later. Its traces were more or less obliterated
when it was ravaged first by the Black Prince in 1355 and again during the wars of
religion.
Market: Tuesday.
Fairs: last Tuesday in each month.

⚔ *SAINT‑SULPICE‑SUR‑LEZE, a Hospitallers' town in a
forest refounded in 1257 by Alphonse de Poitiers, displays most of the features of a
perfect bastide. A fragmentary fresco in its church depicts the Last Judgement.
Fairs: Wednesday in each month.
Festival: last Sunday in August.

⚔ VILLEFRANCHE‑DE‑LAURAGAIS,   founded   by
Alphonse de Poitiers around 1270 and given a charter by Philippe le Bel in 1280,
has a fourteenth‑century church with a gable‑belfry whose glory is two sets of stone
sculptures dating from the fifteenth and sixteenth centuries. The bastide is
renowned today for its cassoulets and its tripe.
Market: Friday.
Cattle fair: last Friday of each month.

Hautes-Garonne

⚔ GALAN sits on a strategic site at a corner of the Lannemezan plateau. A Benedictine priory existed here before the royal bastide was founded in the early fourteenth century and was granted its charter of franchises in 1318. A fortified gateway leads into its criss-crossed streets and half-timbered houses. The sixteenth-century Gothic church has a gable-belfry, two sculpted Gothic entrances and a three-aisled nave. Protestants played havoc here during the wars of religion.
Communal festival: last Sunday in August.

⚔ MAUBOURGET, seat of a Benedictine priory founded in the eleventh century on one of the routes to Santiago de Compostela, commands the confluence of the rivers Adour and Echez. The town retains some vestiges of the fortifications of its bastide, as well as streets set at right angles to each other and a huge central market square. The Romanesque church is older than the bastide, dating back to the eleventh century, though it was restored in the nineteenth. Its cupola was added in the twelfth century and carries an octagonal belfry. Inside are finely sculpted capitals and a statue of Jesus carved in wood in the fifteenth century. Maize, tourism and foie gras are the staple industries of Maubourget.
Patronal festival: Sunday after 15 August (feast of the Assumption).
Communal festival: third Sunday in July.

⚔ RABASTENS-DE-BIGORRE takes its name from the senes-chal Guillaume de Rabastens who founded the bastide in 1306. Its spacious central square with a covered market hall and a nineteenth-century fountain is converged upon by streets crossed at right angles by others. Built of brick and sandstone, the fourteenth-century Gothic church is buttressed and boasts a fourteenth-century Gothic porch, a nave with side aisles and bays and a nineteenth-century belfry.
Cattle market: Monday (some 150,000 calves sold annually).
Fairs: 21–22 January, Monday after Low Sunday, Trinity Sunday, 16 July (feast of Saint Anne), 22 September, 11 November.

⚔ *REJEAUMONT was a bastide founded by the Cistercians in 1285, though today it is a quiet village with a neo-classical seventeenth-century church.
Festival: Sunday following 19 June.

⚔ TOURNAY's streets are set out in a chequerboard plan, surrounding a large central market square. Founded in 1307, the bastide has a church rebuilt in

1850 to incorporate a Gothic porch. The Benedictines have returned, living in a modern abbey and selling ceramics.

Festival: 3 August.

 *TRIE-SUR-BAISE takes its name from the seneschal of Toulouse, Jean de Trie, who founded it in 1322. Its circular boundaries, once fortified, enclose a bastide whose streets follow a regular plan and whose central market square, bordered with arcaded covered walks, is vast. The blocks of the houses are all strictly geometrical, originally built two storeys high and each allotted a garden. Many of its finest houses date from the eighteenth century, numerous older ones having been destroyed when the bastide was set on fire in 1569 during the wars of religion. The former collegiate church, Notre-Dame-des-Neiges is built in the flamboyant Gothic style of the fifteenth century. Patterned on a Latin cross, its gable-belfry (restored in the nineteenth century) rises 60 metres above the entrance, which again displays the flamboyant Gothic style. Unusually for a bastide, the church sits beside the market square and not slightly apart from it.

A few of the fortifications of Trie-sur-Baïse are still in place: a square gateway tower, built of brick, a round defensive tower and a square one. The Carmelites founded a convent here in the fourteenth century, and you can still see its chapel (though the sculpted capitals are now in New York).

Far from being a relic of the past, this bastide has a market which sells more piglets than any other in France, and on the first Tuesday in August the local hippodrome comes to life.

Market: Tuesday.

Fairs: first week of January (foie gras); August, October, December (lambs); 13 December (feast of Saint Lucy, fowl).

Festival: first Sunday in August.

Landes

A U D I G N O N, a staging post on the route to Santiago de Compostela, displays only a few traces of the former fourteenth-century bastide of Careyrot, since in 1441 the lord of Albret set fire to it to chase out the English. The town

boasts a Romanesque church with a lovely fifteenth-century stone reredos.
Patronal festival: 15 August (feast of the Assumption).

☒ *BONNEGARDE, founded in 1279 by King Edward 1 of England, was given to Gaston de Foix in 1342. Little remains of its old pattern, though here stands the ruins of the château of Castera, a windmill of 1305 and a church built in 1898.
Patronal festival: first Sunday in August.

☒ BUANES was founded in 1346, after an act of *paréage* between King Edward 11 of England and Count Pierre 1 de Castelnau. Little remains of the bastide, but the observant visitor can trace its lines, and the water mills hint at its former prosperity. The fourteenth-century church boasts a delicate belfry and a semi-circular apse.
Festival: first Sunday in May.

☒ CACHEN, a former fourteenth-century bastide in the valley of the Gouaneyre, has a nineteenth-century church because the Protestants burned down the original one in 1569.

☒ CAZERES-SUR-L'ADOUR, founded in 1318 by the viscount of Béarn, has preserved its arcaded market square.
Fair: last Saturday of October.
Festival: nearest Sunday to 24 August.

☒ GEAUNE-EN-TURSAN, capital of the hilly region of the Tursan, was founded by Edward 1 of England and Pierre de Castelnau, lord of nearby Castelnau-Tursan, in 1318. The bastide stayed loyal to the English during the Hundred Years War. A massive keep, encorbelled houses in brick and stone and a market square arcaded on three sides are among the attractions of the spot, as well as its fifteenth-century Gothic church, dedicated to Saint John the Baptist, whose huge, buttressed porch of 1452, set on four pillars, rises to become the belfry. The church porch has ogival vaulting, as does the interior. Look out for the capitals, carved with foliage.

Geaune-en-Tursan has lost its walls, and the market hall was demolished in 1880. An Augustinian convent, founded in 1452, was partially wrecked by the Huguenots during the wars of religion. Its lovely Gothic church tower still rises here, topped by a stone belfry, and you can spot some of the vaulting of the ruined nave. Geaune is the centre of the Tursan wine industry.
Market: Thursday.

Fairs: first Thursday in March and September.

Patronal festival: first Sunday in July.

GRENADE-SUR-L'ADOUR, one of several bastides named after celebrated foreign cities, was founded by the English in 1322 and remained English until 1442. During the wars of religion the Protestants attacked and damaged the town. The market square is arcaded and the bastide has preserved some fourteenth- and fifteenth-century houses. Its church, though Gothic in style, dates from 1771.

Market: alternate Mondays.

Fairs: 14 July (Bastille Day), 1 September, first Monday in November, 2 December.

Patronal festival: 26 June.

Communal festival: first Sunday in June.

HASTINGUES, an English bastide founded in 1289 by Jean de Hastings, seneschal of Gascony, on behalf of Edward II, remained loyal to the English until 1451. A Premonstratensian abbey had been founded nearby by the abbey of la Case-Dieu at Auch in 1160, and the foundation was in *paréage* with its abbot. Though not strictly part of the bastide, a visit to their exquisite convent at Arthous is undoubtedly one of the treats of Hastingues.

The bastide itself is set on a defensive ridge above the valley of the Gaves-Réunis close by their confluence with the Adour. The defences were strengthened in the fourteenth century by a town gate, set in earth fortifications. Its square tower still stands, rising above an arched entrance with grooves where once fitted the portcullis.

Although the troops of the Emperor Charles V set fire to part of Hastingues in 1523 and the Huguenots did more damage, it remains splendid, with the main street, some six metres in width, running in a straight line from the town gate as far as the rectangular, arcaded market place. On either side are groups of houses, themselves in regular blocks and separated by narrow lanes (*andrones*) in case of fire. In the market place rise fifteenth- and sixteenth-century houses. At one side stands the parish church of Saint-Sauveur, in its present form dating from the seventeenth century and altered in the eighteenth and nineteenth, though its belfry was built in the fourteenth century. The so-called house of the seneschal, built in the fifteenth century, stands in rue du Centre. Château d'Estrac (seventeenth-century, restored in the nineteenth) takes it name from Bertrand d'Estrac who built it and was a counsellor to the king of Navarre.

Apart from maize, this is sheep country and also produces foie gras, chiefly from ducks.

Patronal festival: Whit Sunday.

Festival: 15 August (feast of the Assumption).

⚅ LABASTIDE-CHALOSSE, as can still be made out, was a circular bastide. Founded in 1327 by Edward II, is was almost completely destroyed during the wars of religion.

⚅ LABASTIDE-D'ARMAGNAC, with its half-timbered houses, is fully described elsewhere in this book. Founded in 1294 to protect the lands of the English from the counts of Foix, it received its charter in 1294. Pastors sent by Calvin from Geneva converted the place to Protestantism, as a result of which it was savaged by Blaise de Montluc. Armagnac is distilled and sold here as are confits and foie gras.
Market: Saturday.
Fairs: third Saturday of January, February, November, December.
Patronal festival: 22 June.

⚅ MIRAMONT-SENSACQ has a Romanesque church with Carolingian font (at Sensacq, where there is also a seventeenth-century château). The church at Miramont boasts a gable-belfry.
Patronal festival: 11 November (feast of Saint Martin of Tours).
Festival: begins second Sunday in August.

⚅ MONTEGUT, in the Midou valley, was founded in 1289 by the seneschal of Gascony on behalf of Edward I. The octagonal tower of its parish church rises from a square base. Although the building is in essence Romanesque, its porch is Gothic. Montégut also boasts some ancient houses.
Communal festival: 6 August.

⚅ MONTFORT-EN-CHALOSSE is a bastide created by the English in the thirteenth century to command the central Chalosse region, and from here you can see not only stretches of the Landes forest but also the Pyrenees. The bastide was set around a Romanesque church built by the abbey of Divielle. The choir and the nave of the church are still Romanesque, but the rest, including its mighty square tower, dates from the fifteenth century. It houses a fifteenth-century statue of the Virgin.
Market: Friday.
Fairs: alternate Fridays, with larger fairs in February, May, September, December.
Festival: Sunday after 30 July.

⚅ *PIMBO is served by the church of Saint Bartholomew which was built by the Benedictines.

Patronal festival: 24 August (feast of Saint Bartholomew).

⚑ SAINT‑GEOURS‑D'AURIBAT, set in woodlands beside the River Louts, is an English bastide with a fountain dedicated to Saint George. Festival: 24 April.

⚑ SAINT‑JUSTIN, founded by the Knights Hospitallers in *paréage* with the viscount of Marsan, has preserved some of its surrounding wall and towers. The arcaded market place with its half‑timbered houses is shaded by lime trees. The thirteenth‑century church, restored in the nineteenth century, houses a crucifix of 1600.
Market: Monday.
Fairs: first Monday of January – May and December; also 5 January, 23 and 24 July.
Communal festival: around 14 July (Bastille Day).

⚑ SARRON, in the valley of the Lées, bears little trace today of the former bastide.
Communal festival: 25 November.

⚑ *SORDE‑L'ABBAYE, overlooking the confluence of the Po and the Oloron is described elsewhere in this book.
Patronal festival: last Sunday in August.

Lot

⚑ BEAUREGARD is one of the bastides which grew out of a founda‑ tion of the Knights *Templars. Its Romanesque parish church of Saint Laurence (restored in the nineteenth century) belonged to them and after their disgrace passed into the hands of the Knights Hospitallers. Beauregard also has a fourteenth‑ century church which shelters a relic of Saint John.

Initially the possession of the abbot of Marcilhac, after a dispute with the

consuls in the fourteenth century, the bastide was bought from him by the king.
Fairs: 27th of each month.
Patronal Festival: 15 August (feast of the Assumption).
Communal festival: first Sunday in September.

BRETENOUX in the Cère valley, known as Villafranca when the lord of Castelnau founded the bastide, has a market place surrounded by arcades. Its town hall was built in the fifteenth century. Some of the ramparts are still intact. The eighteenth-century church in the cemetery contains an early sixteenth-century polychrome statue of the Virgin.
Market: Monday.
Fairs: 26th of each month.
Patronal festival: second Sunday in September.

*CASTELNAU-MONTRATIER, is described in detail on other pages.
Market: second Tuesday of each month.
Patronal festival: 11 November (feast of Saint Martin of Tours).

LABASTIDE-MURAT, which is set on one of the highest parts of the Gramat plateau, took the name of Joachim Murat in 1836, having formerly been known as Labastide-Fortanière. His birthplace there is a humble farmer's home, the lower storey used for cattle, the upper for living, the whole built out of roughly-hewn stones. Murat built here a château and paid for a church. A museum is devoted to him.
MARKET: fourth Monday of each month.
Fairs: second Monday of each month.
Patronal festival: second Sunday in August.

*MONTCABRIER is described elsewhere in these pages.
Fairs: Sunday after 26 August, 11 October, 24 November.
Patronal festival: Sunday after 26th August.

*MONTFAUCON has old houses and a market hall, as well as a fifteenth-century church.
Patronal festival: 24 August, (feast of Saint Bartholomew).

PUYBRUN, a bastide created in the thirteenth century by Philippe le Hardi and the Cistercian abbot of Dalon, received its charter of customs in 1283. Known then as Labastide-de-Tauriac, it took the name Puybrun ('brown hill') in 1310. Its pattern still follows the regular one of a bastide, and its church dates from the thirteenth and fourteenth centuries, though it was restored in the eighteenth.

Fairs: 10th and 27th of each month.

Patronal festival: last Sunday in July.

Lot-et-Garonne

BEAUVILLE is set on a hill overlooking the Séoune. The contours of this hill determined the shape of the fourteenth-century ramparts, traces of which remain. At the heart of the bastide is a small, arcaded market place and some half-timbered houses. The fourteenth-century Gothic church has a Renaissance porch and a belfry in the form of a pyramid, once evidently serving as a defensive tower. Its sixteenth-century château is based on an earlier one, built in the thirteenth century. This is now a holiday town, with water sports and concerts.

Market: Sunday after 15 June; 15 November.

Communal festival: 16 August (feast of Saint Roch).

CASTELNAU-SUR-GUPIE developed into a bastide, created by the English, from a *castelnau* which was the seat of a commandery of the Knights of Hospitallers. Its fifteenth-century church, with a Romanesque porch and a sixteenth-century nave, served as their chapel.

Patronal festival: third Sunday in June.

Communal festival: first Sunday in September.

CASTELNAUD-DE-GRATECAMBE, founded by Alphonse de Poitiers in 1272 on a Roman Road south of Manflanquin, was scarcely recognizable as a bastide after the wars of religion, when the church was destroyed (hence the modern one here today).

Patronal festival: feast of Corpus Christi.

*CASTILLONNES, founded by Alphonse de Poitiers in 1259, is in part described on other pages. Some of the the ramparts remain here. The thirteenth-century church was completely restored in the nineteenth century.
Market: Tuesday.
Fairs: third Tuesday of each month; 4 January.

CAUDECOSTE in the valley of the Garonne is a circular bastide whose market place still retains its arcades. The Gothic church dates from the nineteenth century.
Patronal festival: Sunday after 22 July, unless 22 July happens to be a Sunday.

*DAMAZAN, described elsewhere in this book, exploits its eight-hectare lake for tourism.
Market: Sunday.
Fair: first Wednesday of each month.
Festival: penultimate Sunday in September.

*DURANCE was founded by the English King Edward II in 1320. North of the bastide are the ruins of a priory built by the Premonstratensians in the thirteenth century.
Fairs: 7 January, 1 May, 12 June, 4 August, 22 September, 12 November.
Patronal festival: 3 August.

*FRANCESCAS, a thirteenth-century bastide, has a thirteenth-century church, restored in the nineteenth century. It was a fief of the family La Hire, one of whose members was a companion of Joan of Arc and lived in a fifteenth-century house here.
Fairs: starting eight days before Lent: others on 8 July, 9 September, 11 November and 28 December.

*LABASTIDE-CASTEL-AMOUROUX, founded by Alphonse de Poitiers in 1269 and given its charter of rights and privileges in 1287, is chiefly remarkable for its thirteenth-century church, described elsewhere in this book.
Patronal festival: 15 August (feast of the Assumption).

*LAMONTJOIE, has a fifteenth-century church dedicated to Saint Louis enshrining part of his hand, a gift to the bastide from Philippe le Bel when he issued its charter of customs in 1299. The reliquary, in gilded and enamelled bronze, is an imaginary bust of the monarch and saint.

Patronal festival: 15 August (feast of the Assumption).
Communal festival: feast of the Ascension.

⚌   *LAPARADE offers panoramas of the valleys of the Lot and the Torque. Seventeenth-century half-timbered houses line rue du 8 Mai 945. A French foundation, Laparade became English in 1318 and French again in 1437. Accepting the tenets of the Reformation, its citizens were punished in 1622 when Louis XIII had their fortifications demolished.
Patronal festival: Sunday after Easter.

⚌   *LA SAUVETAT-DU-DROPT, described elsewhere in the text, was taken by the *croquants in 1637. They were put down by the Duc de Valette, who had 1500 of them slaughtered, as well as setting fire to part of the bastide.
Fairs: 22 January, 23 April, Saturday after first Sunday in August, Tuesday before 15 September, 28 October, 30 November.
Patronal festival: first Sunday in August.

⚌   *LAVARDAC, which is decribed elsewhere in this book, suffered much destruction during the wars of religion, and especially in 1621.
Fairs: 17 January, 10 July, 6 August, 11 November.
Patronal festival: 15 August (feast of the Assumption).

⚌   LE TEMPLE-SUR-LOT, was originally a village that had grown up around a commandery of the Knights *Templars. At their suppression it passed into the hand of the Knights Hospitallers who in 1320 entered into an act of paréage with King Edward II of England to transform the place into a bastide, with the intention of countering the influence of the nearby French bastide of Saint-Sardos (above). Although the bastide has disappeared, the splendid late fifteenth century commandery of the Hospitallers still stands, built out of brick, with round and square towers. The parish church (restored in the nineteenth century) served as their chapel.
Patronal festival: feast of the Ascension.

⚌   MONCLAR-D'AGENAIS, founded by Alphonse de Poitiers in 1256, has a small market place with the traditional arcades of a bastide. Its late Gothic church dates from the early sixteenth century.
Fairs: 22 January, the Saturday before Lent, around Palm Sunday, around 15 August (feast of the Assumption), various Saturdays during the other months of the year.
Patronal festival: first Sunday in June.

*MONFLANQUIN, a remarkably well preserved bastide exten/sively described elsewhere in this book, is set on a 180/metre hill. Only the façade of the church of Notre/Dame has preserved its fifteenth century Gothic form, for the nave and choir were destroyed during the wars of religion and rebuilt in 1673. The bastide is well equipped for tourists.

Market: Wednesdays and Saturdays, early July to early September.

Fairs: first Saturday of most months.

*PUYMIROL, set high above the Séoune valley, was taken in 1574 by the Protestants, who held on to it for the rest of the century. In consequence Louis XIII had most of its ramparts demolished.

Fairs: first Friday of each month.

Patronal festival: last Sunday in August.

Communal festival: 14 July (Bastille Day).

*SAINT/PASTOUR's oldest part is its parish church, though this was mostly rebuilt in the late fifteenth century, the vaulting finished in 1502. Its doorway is Renaissance.

Patronal festival: Low Sunday.

Communal festivals: 14 July (Bastille Day); last Sunday in August.

*SAINT/SARDOS was the scene in 1323 of an incident which helped to spark off the Hundred Years' War. (see chapter 4).

Fairs: 14 February, 2 April, 19 July, 20 August, 17 September, 20 November.

Patronal and communal festivals: Sunday after feast of Corpus Christi.

TOURNON/D'AGENAIS, founded on a plateau by Alphonse de Poitiers in 1270, was fortified by Edward 1 of England in 1282. The road up to the bastide twists beside his ramparts. The central market square is bordered with arcaded houses. Although the church is modern, the old one destroyed during the wars of religion, Tournon/d'Agenais boasts both stone and half/timbered dwellings.

Fairs: third Monday of each month.

Patronal festival: Sunday after 23 August.

Communal festival: second Sunday in July.

*VIANNE, a well/preserved English bastide founded in 1284, is fully described in Chapter 4.

Fair: 26 November.

Communal festival: last Sunday in July.

⚔ VILLEFRANCHE-DU-QUEYRAN, a bastide founded in the thirteenth century, was taken by the English in 1340 and occupied by the Protestants in 1569. Much of the former bastide has disappeared, but the market hall is here and a fifteenth-century church. The Romanesque church of Saint-Savin, a kilometre from the bastide, though partly ruined, is well worth a visit, especially to see its 27 carved capitals, some depicting foliage, others biblical scenes.

Fairs: 28th of each month.

Communal festival: second Sunday in June.

⚔ *VILLENEUVE-SUR-LOT, one of Alphonse de Poitiers's major foundations and superbly situated on either side of the River Lot where once were huge forests, is extensively described elsewhere in this book, save for the church of Saint Stephen and the town hall (see below). Evidence of a Gallo-Roman settlement is to be seen in the round Gaulish tower still standing in the suburb of Eysses.

The charter of the bastide was long, 46 articles in all. In spite of many attacks, the bastide survived intact both the Hundred Years War and the wars of religion. During the Fronde its tall thirteenth century *porte de Paris* even survived 19 assaults by cannon. As an indication of the turbulence of past times, the house known as the *maison de Marguérite de Valois* is so called not because she lived there but because it was the seat of her council of war. The Revolution expelled from Villeneuve-sur-Lot a convent of the Poor Clares, whose elegant home, built in the classical style overlooking the river, is now the town hall.

Saint Stephen (Saint-Etienne), parish church of the left bank and these days surrounded by plane trees, predates the bastide, dating back to the twelfth century, but its present form is that of a Gothic church restored in the seventeenth century. Its lierne vaulting, with pendentives, is delicate, arches spreading upwards from pilas-ters, the nave reaching to a small, tall and delicately vaulted apse. Its steeple is pierced with four round arches, carrying four differently sized bells.

Apart from its attractions as an urban ensemble, Villeneuve-sur-Lot is an animated place. Riverboats and skiffs ply the Lot, and there is a racecourse in operation during the summer. Decorated floats parade the streets to honour Saint Roch and Saint Fiacre at the end of June and the beginning of July. This is a region given to confits of duck served with cèpe mushrooms and truffled foie gras, while the surrounding orchards and market gardens, evidence of the way a bastide trans-formed a forest into fertile land, produce plums which, when dried, become the celebrated *pruneaux d'Agen*.

Market: Wednesday, Saturday.

Fairs: second and fourth Tuesday in each month; 3 February, 20 May (agricultural

fair), 20 July, end August (lasting 8 days), 1 September, 28 December (for foie gras and confits).
Festival; end June and beginning of July (feasts of Saint Roch and Saint Fiacre).

*VILLEREAL, set on a hill on the left bank of the River Dropt and fully described on other pages of this book, was founded on a site inhabited by prehistoric people, as numerous dolmens and tumuli in the region reveal. Cereals, grapes and plums are the principal products of the region. Villeréal has a race-course.
Market: Wednesday.
Fairs: 17 January; Saturday before Shrove Tuesday, third Saturday in Lent, Easter Saturday, day before Whit Sunday; 23 April, 25 June, 16 August, 30 September, 31 October, 21 November and Christmas Eve.

Pyrénées-Atlantiques

AINHOA was founded in the thirteenth century by the Premonstraten-sian monks of Saint-Sauveur at Urdax and for centuries protected pilgrims on the way to Spain and Santiago de Compostela. Its houses are set out in regular parcels. The main square of Aïnhoa is overlooked by the medieval church (which was enlarged in the sixteenth century) and dominated by the belfry, which starts off square, becomes octagonal as it rises and ends with a slate-covered steeple. The main street is flanked with half-timbered houses, painted green and red.
Patronal festival: 15 August (feast of the Assumption).

BELLOCQ, now known through amalgamation with other villages by its composite name Puyoô-Bellocq-Ramous, was the site of a château (now in ruins, though enough remains to evoke its past) which passed into the hands of Gaston *Fébus. He was responsible for building the bastide of Bellocq. The parish church of Notre-Dame-de l'Assomption has two lovely porches, that on the south side dating from the thirteenth century, the richly carved one on the west dating from the late fifteenth century.

Patronal festival: 15 August (feast of the Assumption).

⊠ BRUGES, now Bruges-Capbis-Mifaget, was founded in the winter of 1357–8 by Bertrand de Puyols on behalf of Gaston *Fébus and received its charter of customs around 1360. Its market place is still arcaded; the Gothic parish church was built in the first half of the sixteenth century; and the bastide's water mills are still there.

Patronal festival: 15 August (feast of the Assumption).

⊠ GARLIN still preserves streets running at right angles to each other and the central market place of the bastide founded in 1302. Its Gothic church, dedicated to Saint John the Baptist, was built in 1861. This bastide looks out towards the Pyrenees.

Market: alternate Wednesdays.

Communal festival: last Sunday in July.

Patronal festival: 26 June.

⊠ LABASTIDE-CLAIRANCE, on the banks of the Joyeuse at its highest navigable point, was founded in 1314 by Louis x the Quarrelsome, king of France and Navarre. Situating his bastide at the northern limits of Navarre with the intention of profiting from the river trade with Bayonne, Louis peopled his new town with immigrants from Bigorre. In consequence the inhabitants still speak Gascon in what is Basque country.

Laid out in chequerboard fashion, its streets centre on the market place, whose houses have stone arcades. Other half-timbered houses, some encorbelled, some with sculpted lintels, also grace Labastide-Clairance.

Typically, the church is set away from the market place, here a long way off as if the house of God wished to have no truck with the den of thieves on market day. What is rare in a present-day bastide is that the building is still surrounded by its extensive graveyard, witnessed to by funeral slabs. The church itself is Gothic, restored in the seventeenth and eighteenth centuries, with a fine porch and sculpted arches. Beyond it is the graveyard of the Jewish community which took refuge here in the seventeenth and eighteenth centuries, driven from Spain by the Inquisition. A pleasing memory is that the people of this bastide resisted any attempt to get rid of their Jewish doctor when the Paris parlement forbade Jews to practise medicine. The communal wash house is by the former port.

Patronal festival: 15 August (feast of the Assumption).

⚜ LABASTIDE-VILLEFRANCHE was founded by Gaston Fébus in the fourteenth century as a bulwark against the English settled in Bayonne. Its square, fourteenth-century keep is consequently known as the Tour Fébus. The medieval church has a belfry which is also square.
Market: Monday.
Fairs: Monday before Lent, Easter Monday, Whit Monday, last Monday in September.
Patronal festival: 15 August (feast of the Ascension).

⚜ LESTELLE-BETHARRAM, includes the bastide of Lestelle which Viscount Gaston de Foix of Béarn founded in 1335. Straight streets run off from the central market square, criss-crossed regularly by others. Lestelle's church houses a baroque reredos illustrating the life of its patron, Saint John the Baptist.
Patronal festival: 24 June (feast of Saint John the Baptist).

⚜ MAULEON-LICHARRE in its fortress-like upper town incor-porates a fourteenth-century French bastide, with a rectangular market place surrounded by arcades. Its earlier fortress is now a ruin. The bastide once domi-nated the valley of the Saison, passing into the hands of the English in 1307 and not relinquished by them until 1449.
Market: Tuesday morning.

⚜ NAVARRENX, which was founded in the eleventh century, became a bastide in 1316. After Jeanne d'Albret, the poet and mother of Henri IV, was converted to Calvinism, Navarrenx became a refuge of Huguenots. A Catholic army laid siege to the town on 24 May, 1569, and had failed to capture it by the beginning of July when a Protestant army arrived, defeated the Catholic troops and had their leaders executed in the bastide. Troops of Louis XIII also laid siege to Navarrenx in 1620, and the aged Baron d'Arros, who had rallied the Huguenots in 1569, this time capitulated after a few days.

The layout of the town still follows for the most part that of the old bastide, with its central market place and streets laid out at right angles to each other. The fortifications include *porte Saint-Antoine*, which once had a portcullis and whose upper storeys served in the past as a prison and a guard-house. The *porte de France* has long since disappeared, but the bastion of Mont-Livet which guarded it still stands, restored in 1856. Two other bastions protect the heart of Navarrenx. In the place de la Mairie rises the Gothic church of Saint-Germain, built between 1551 and 1562, its left aisle added only in 1852.

Navarrenx now is a popular holiday centre, hosting a renowned salmon fishing contest on the banks of the Oloron from April to July.

Market: Tuesday.

Fairs: Ash Wednesday, Wednesday before Palm Sunday, third Wednesday in September, and 8 and 12 December.

Festivals: during the last fortnight of June; second Sunday in August.

 NAY-BOURDETTES occupies the site of a village founded by the monks of Sainte-Christine du Somport at the beginning of the twelfth century. Marguérite, viscountess of Béarn, founded a bastide on the spot in 1302. Prospering on textiles, Nay boasted 108 hearths in 1385. It was seriously damaged by fire in 1543 and was rebuilt retaining the former criss-cross pattern of its streets and its arcaded market place.

Its streets converge on the arcaded place de la République. No. 15 is a sixteenth-century house now known as the *maison de Jeanne d'Albret*, a Renaissance building three storeys high, its inner courtyard displaying three stages of vaulted galleries, its rooms Renaissance chimneys. The River Pau was utilized to drive water mills, which still stand. The Gothic parish church, with its powerful belfry which starts off square and finishes octagonal, was built in the fifteenth century and rebuilt in the flamboyant Gothic style after the fire of 1543. Lierne vaulted, with entrancing pendentives and capitals, its font was sculpted in the sixteenth century, its other furnishings deriving from the seventeenth and eighteenth centuries. Note the fine south porch.

Market: Tuesday.

Fair: begins on the first Wednesday in Lent and lasts for three days.

Communal festival: last fortnight in August.

Tarn

 BRIATEXTE was founded beside the River Dadou in the second half of the 1280s by the seneschal of Gascony, Simon Brisetête, on behalf of King Philippe le Bel. Its market square is arcaded, and an old windmill still sits beside the river. Until 1622 the bastide was fortified, but after the duke of Vendôme had recaptured it from the Protestants in 1622 the fortifications were razed on the orders of Louis XIII. The parish church of Notre-Dame dates from 1846.

Market: Tuesday.

Fairs: Monday before Easter, 24 August, Monday before 1 November (All Saints' Day).

Patronal festival: 15 August (feast of the Assumption).

*CASTELNAU-DE-LEVIS was founded in 1235 by Sicard I d'Alaman on behalf of Count Raymond VII of Toulouse in order to shelter a population at risk because of the depredations of Simon de Montfort (see Chapter 1), and no doubt because Raymond also wanted a bastion against Albi, which had passed into the hands of the French monarchy at the Treaty of Meaux in 1229. Castelnau-de-Lévis received its charter of customs in 1256. The hilltop bastide has views over the Tarn valley, and is guarded by a ruined thirteenth-century château and a powerful double-storeyed watchtower. Its church was built from the thirteenth to the fifteenth centuries and as befits one in a defensive bastide has a fortified belfry. Most of its furnishings date from the fifteenth and sixteenth centuries.

A good part of the château was demolished between 1820 and 1909, its stones used elsewhere.

Patronal festival: 24 August.

Communal festival: begins last Sunday in April.

CASTELNAU-DE-MONTMIRAL, one of the earliest bastides, founded by Raymond VII of Toulouse shortly after Cordes (see below), rests on a hilltop site and was fortified in the fourteenth century (a few vestiges remain). The market place is arcaded, one of its houses dated 1600. Other houses in this bastide have sweet Gothic or Renaissance windows. Castelnau-de-Montmiral is served by a fifteenth-century Gothic church with a decorated porch, sheltering a remarkable reliquary-cross, encrusted in the fourteenth century with some 450 precious stones of which 310 are still in place.

Fairs: 25 January, 15 February, 25 March, second Monday after Easter, 16 May, 9 June, 10 July, 1 August, 20 August, 9 September, 15 October, 19 November, 28 December.

Patronal festival: 15 August (feast of the Assumption).

*CORDES, built on the Puech de Mordagne, an exceptional site over the Cérou valley, is remarkable and most of it is described elsewhere in this book. Few bastides can compete with the ability of this one to transport the visitor back into the past. In the Middle Ages two hospices sheltered pilgrims. La Capelette, whose present form dates from 1511, was the chapel of the hospice of Saint James, founded in the early fourteenth century for pilgrims to Santiago de Compostela. The second hospice, l'hôpital des Trinitaires, was destroyed by Huguenots in 1568, but the monks then moved to the Grand'Rue, where they built a convent with its chapel and cloister. The whole ensemble was sold during the Revolution, and today you can visit only the cloister, the rest having been converted into houses.

As is recounted elsewhere in these pages, Cordes fell on hard times and was a desolate spot until the twentieth century.

Market: Saturday morning.

Fairs: second Saturday in January, first Saturday in February, Thursday after Easter, 29 May, 24 June, last Saturday in July, 25 August, first Saturday in October, 25 November. Christmas Eve.

Festival: feast of the Grand Fauconnier, 14 July (Bastille Day), among others.

🝢 *LABASTIDE-DE-LEVIS, founded by Amaury de Montfort, retains some of its old chequerboard patterned streets and an arcaded central square. The Gothic church of Saint Blaise, built in the fifteenth and sixteenth centuries, has a splendid belfry-doorway, ogival vaulting and a fifteenth century font.

Patronal festival: 3 February.

🝢 *LISLE-SUR-TARN, whose oldest quarters, built out of brick, are described elsewhere in this book, is notable for its *pontents*, arched ones for instance in rue du Musée, others simply held up on beams as in rue de la Solitude.

Market: Sunday.

Fairs: 22 January, first Thursday in Lent, 11 June, 28 August, 20 October, 30 November, 12 December.

🝢 *PAMPELONNE is another of those bastides such as Cordes and Bruges which were named after an important foreign city. Founded by the French, it was captured by the English during the Hundred Years War. Becoming Prot-estant, the bastide was chastized by Louis XIII, who destroyed its fortifications and the thirteenth-century château de Thuriès, which are now evocative ruins.

The church of 1846 shelters a seventeenth-century reredos.

Fairs: first Wednesday of each month.

Patronal festival: 8 September.

Communal festival: first Sunday in August.

*R E A L M O N T was founded in 1272 on behalf of Philippe le Hardi by the seneschal of Carcassonne, Guillaume de Cohardon, with the intention of stamping out the Cathars (see Chapter 1). In 1561 it became a Protestant stronghold which revolted in the 1620s against the religious policies of Louis XIII. Defeated, the Protestants saw their ramparts demolished in 1623. In the old town the bastide's market place is still arcaded. Here too is a seventeenth-century fountain and a seventeenth-century church which was enlarged in 1777.

Market: (for rabbits, fowl and pink garlic).

Fairs: first and third Wednesdays of each month, 1 May, Wednesdays before Palm Sunday and Christmas.

Tarn-et-Garonne

 BEAUMONT-DE-LOMAGNE, founded in 1276 by the Cistercian abbot of Grand-Selve in *paréage* with Eustache de Beaumarchais, received its charter of rights and duties from Philippe le Hardi three years later. Here in 1430 the bishop of Montauban took refuge when the English drove him from his see. In 1580 the bastide became a shelter for Huguenots.

Its arcaded market place, surrounded by haromonious seventeenth- and eighteenth century houses, surrounds a splendid wooden market hall, built in the fourteenth century and some 1500 square metres in area. The square also has a statue of the mathematician Pierre Fermat, who was born at Beaumont-de-Lomagne in 1601 and invented differential calculus. Not far away is the parish church of Notre-Dame, a powerful thirteenth- and fourteenth-century building with a fifteenth-century octagonal belfry. The eighteenth-century stalls inside the church came from the abbey of Grand-Selve.

Initially the bastide, which lies in the valley of the Gimone, was named Beaumont-sur-Gimone.

Market: Wednesday and Saturday, July to February (for the local garlic; capons and turkeys in December).

Communal festival: 15 August (feast of the Assumption).

CASTELSAGRAT, founded by Alphonse de Poitiers in 1270, was bitterly fought over during the Hundred Years War. Richelieu had its ramparts demolished. In part described on other pages of this book, it is blessed with a parish church, set at an angle to the market place, inside which is a fine reredos, sculpted in 1669 by Pierre Affre, which came from the collegiate church of Saint Raymond in Toulouse.

Patronal festival: 15 August (feast of the Assumption).

DUNES, which the seneschal of Agenais and Quercy, Philippe de Villefavreuse, along with Raymond Bernard de Durfort, founded on behalf of Alphonse de Poitiers around 1270, has preserved parts of its fortifications and an arcaded market place surrounded by seventeenth- and eighteenth-century houses. A new town hall insinuated itself into the market hall in the 1940s. The church of Saint Mary Magdalen was begun in the fourteenth century, though only the porch remains from this era: the rest dates from the sixteenth and seventeenth centuries. Bishop Hérard of Conques who reigned from 1521 to 1544 had the masons engrave his coat of arms on the keystone of the apse. Though the belfry is patterned on the ancient Toulouse style, it was built only in 1848.

Festival: 15 August.

LAUZERTE is exquisitely situated amidst vineyards and orchards, and is washed by the streams of the Petite Barguelone, the Séoune and the Lendou. Even when the bastide was occupied by the English during the Hundred Years War, many of its citizens remained resolutely French. One legend relates that a poor widow watched the English garrison leave Lauzerte to make a foray in surrounding countryside and counted out each soldier with chestnuts. When the last had left, the widow alerted her companions, who slammed shut the gates and liberated the town.

Two fine churches grace the bastide. Built in the sixteenth and seventeenth centuries, Saint-Barthélemy has a nineteenth-century façade and ogival vaulting. It houses a seventeenth-century baroque reredos. An even finer reredos of the same epoch is in the nearby seventeenth-century Carmelite church.

Fairs: first Monday of each month.

Patronal festival of Saint Bartholomew: 16 July.

Flea market: 15 August (feast of the Assumption).

MONTAUBAN at its heart is an outstanding bastide, the market place entirely rebuilt in the seventeenth century. Once the bastion of the northernmost point of the county of Toulouse, the town became a rallying place for Huguenots.

Market: Saturday.

Festivals: throughout the summer months.

*MONTPEZAT-DE-QUERCY is described elsewhere in these pages.

Fair: fourth Sunday in September (agricultural show). Outside the town is a leisure park.

Festival: feast of the Ascension, for 3 days.

*NEGREPELISSE, which received its charter from Philippe le Hardi in 1285, saw its church ruined by the troops of Louis XIII in 1622. The present church, dedicated to Saint Peter, dates from the nineteenth century. The bastide has an arcaded market place.

Market: Wednesday.

Fairs: second Tuesday in September (agricultural fair): 21 October.

Communal festival: last Sunday in July.

REALVILLE, founded in 1310 by Philippe le Bel, centres on the place Nationale, where the arcades of its sixteenth- and seventeenth-century houses rise on wooden pillars. The seventeenth-century church (with a nineteenth-century belfry) is dedicated to Saint John the Baptist.

Festivals: 24 June, (feast of Saint John the Baptist); end of September (autumn festival).

VALENCE-D'AGEN, a bastide founded by King Edward I of England in 1283 in the valley of the Garonne, is laid out in a chequerboard plan, has an arcaded market place and two communal wash houses (one in the allée des Fontaines, the other in rue Saint-Bernard). The Gothic church of the Nativity was built in the nineteenth century.

Market: Wednesday.

Fair: December (fowl); January (foie gras).

VERFEIL-SUR-SEYE, founded in 1250 by Alphonse de Poitiers, suffered cruelly in subsequent centuries and especially during the wars of religion. Yet its market place has preserved the medieval market hall (restored in the nineteenth century), which rises on stone pillars, and a row of arcades on one side of the square. The eighteenth-century church of Saint Peter in Chains has a baroque altar brought here from the former abbey of Beaulieu-en-Rouergue. Festival: second Sunday in August.

Bibliography

RENÉ ARTIGAUT, *Découvrir Le Tarn*, Jacques Mas 1986

SYLVIE ASSASSIN, BARTHÉLÉMY DUMONS, PHILIPPE GISCLARD AND NATHALIE PRAT, *Les Bastides de Lomagne*, Diagram Editeur 1990

JEAN-LUC AUBARDIER, Michel Binet and Jean-Pierre Bouchard, *Les Bastides du Périgord*, Ouest France 1989

JEAN BARTHE, *Guide des Bastides du Sud du Périgord et du Nord de l'Agenais*, Collection du Centre d'Action Touristique de la Région de Bergerac 1988

JAMES BENTLEY, *A Guide to the Dordogne*, Viking Penguin 1985

JAMES BENTLEY, *The Way of Saint James: a pilgrimage to Santiago de Compostela*, Pavilion Books 1992

GILLES BERNARD, *Les Bastides du Sud-Ouest*, Diagram Editeur 1990

GILLES BERNARD AND GUY CAVAGNAC, *Villefranche de Rouerge. Histoire et Génie du Lieu*, Privat 1991

CLAUDE AND QUITTERIE CALMETTES, *Bastides en Rouerque*, Editions du Beffroi 1990

FRANÇOIS DIVORNE, BERNARD GENDRE, BRUNO LAVERGNE AND PHILIPPE PANERAI, *Essai sur le Régularité. Les Bastides d'Aquitaine, du Bas-Languedoc et du Béarn*, AAM Editions 1985

JACQUES DUBOURG, *Histoire des Bastides d'Aquitaine*, Sud Ouest 1991

JACQUES DUBOURG AND RAY DELVERT, *Connaître les Bastides du Lot-et-Garonne*, Sud Ouest 1991

DANIELLE MAILLARD (ed.), *Languedoc Roussillon*, Fernand Nathan 1981

EMMANUEL LE ROY LADURIE, *Histoire du Languedoc*, Presses Universitaires de France (4th edn) 1982

EMMANUEL LE ROY LADURIE, *Montaillou*, tr. Barbara Bray, Penguin Books 1980

Bibliography

HERBERT LASSERE, *La Bastide et le Canton de Villeréal*, Alain Sanchez 1985

ALAIN LAURET et al., *Bastides. Villes Nouvelles du Moyen Age*, Editions Milan 1988

GUY MERGOIL, *Le Rouerque*, Privat 1982

Monuments Historiques, No.158 Aout–Septembre 1988, 'Les Bastides'

JEAN-MARIE MARTIN, *Visitez Domme*, Sud Ouest 1988

JEAN-MARIE MARTIN, *Visitez Monpazier*, Sud Ouest 1989

PIERRE MINVIELLE, *Pays Basque Béarn*, Fernand Nathan 1985

FERNAND NEIL, *Albigeois et Cathares*, Presses Universitaires de France (9th edn) 1979

JEAN-PIERRE PANOUILLÉ, *The City of Carcassonne*, Ouest France/Caisse Nationale des Monuments Historiques et des Sites 1984

ANDRÉ ROULLAND, *Histoire des Bastides. Un guide pour parcourir ces cités du Sud-Ouest*, Editions de l'Université et de l'Enseignment Moderne n.d

JEAN-MARC SOYEZ, *Quand les Anglais vendangeaint l'Aquitaine. D'Aliénor à Jeanne d'Arc*, Fayard 1978

MARIE-HUMBERT VICAIRE, *Saint Dominique en Lauragais*, Editions Saint-Paul Fribourg (2nd edn) 1975

Index